Copy 2,

SETTLEMENT UNDER
THE CIVIL PROCEDURE RULES

Litigation Library

 DENTON WILDE SAPTE
FIVE CHANCERY LANE
CLIFFORD'S INN
LONDON
EC4A 1BU

AUSTRALIA
LBC Information Services
Sydney

CANADA AND USA
Carswell
Toronto

NEW ZEALAND
Brooker's
Auckland

SINGAPORE AND MALAYSIA
Sweet & Maxwell Asia
Singapore and Kuala Lumpur

SETTLEMENT UNDER
THE CIVIL PROCEDURE RULES

by

David Foskett, Q.C., LL.B., F.C.I.Arb.,
of Gray's Inn, Barrister
and of the Midland and Oxford Circuit
a Recorder

LONDON
SWEET & MAXWELL
1999

Published in 1999 by
Sweet & Maxwell Limited of
100 Avenue Road, Swiss Cottage, London NW3 3PF
(http://www.smlawpub.co.uk)
Typeset by Dataword Services Limited, Chilcompton
Printed and bound in Great Britain by
Butler & Tanner Ltd, Frome and London

No natural forests were destroyed to make this product;
only farmed timber was used and replanted

A CIP catalogue record for this book
is available from the British Library.

ISBN 0421-682507

To

My Colleagues on the Civil Procedure Rule Committee

The long-suffering drafting team

and the extremely patient Minute-takers

The golden rule is that there are no golden rules.

Man and Superman (1903) "Maxims for Revolutionists: The Golden Rule"

George Bernard Shaw

FOREWORD

Under the Civil Procedure Rules offers to settle have become one of the most important elements of the civil justice system. The message of the new regime is that you should not be involved in litigation except as a last resort. Protocols will assist in bringing this about.

However, disputes cannot be avoided. What is required is to resolve the disputes when they arise expeditiously and in a sensible and reasonable way. The new rules should help to achieve this. They will enable the parties to take steps to ensure that they can obtain disclosure so as to form a realistic assessment of the merits of a case without litigation. Both sides will be in a position to make realistic offers to settle without having to commence proceedings. A well judged offer to settle should be the turning point in most disputes.

However, to make such an offer will involve a detailed knowledge and understanding of the rules. The same is true of the emphasis which is now placed on ADR. A mistake could have serious repercussions in the form of adverse orders for costs and interest. This is why I am particularly pleased that David Foskett has written this excellent commentary on making settlements under the new rules. He knows the rules as to settlement intimately. This is because he was one of their principal architects. This book provides practitioners with the information they need to make the best use of their new tools. I congratulate David Foskett on this excellent and comprehensive work which I know will be of immense value to practitioners.

The Right Honourable the Lord Woolf
Master of the Rolls

PREFACE

Two options were available when considering how to make a written contribution concerning the likely practice of settlement under the new rules: the first was to produce a supplement to the fourth edition of *The Law and Practice of Compromise*; the second was to produce a "one-off" introduction to those parts of the Civil Procedure Rules, particularly Part 36, that would be of importance in the new system. The latter approach was felt to be of greater general assistance than the former. This short book is the result of that decision.

In his Foreword to the Civil Procedure Rules the Lord Chancellor, Lord Irvine of Lairg, said that "the changes being introduced in April are as much changes of culture as they are changes in the Rules themselves" and that "we must see this as the beginning, not the end, of the process of change." In this introduction to and analysis of Part 36 I have, where relevant, tried to convey the philosophy underpinning the *Access to Justice* reforms so that its provisions can be seen properly within that framework. Part 36 is merely one part, albeit an important part, of the new structure. The practice of settlement and dispute resolution in the context of the new case-managed system of civil justice will emerge more clearly as that system itself becomes established.

In those parts of the book where I have offered thoughts on how certain issues mights be resolved, I do wish to emphasize that they are inevitably somewhat provisional and, more importantly, entirely personal. In accordance with the intention behind the use of the words "new procedural code" in the very first rule of the Civil Procedure Rules, I have tried to keep reference to previous authority to a minimum. Inevitably, though, certainly at this stage in the process of becoming acclimatised to the new culture, some reference to previous practice and authority is necessary if only to illustrate the changes made.

I would like to express my appreciation to Sir Richard Scott, the Vice-Chancellor, for permitting me a "fast-track" to the emerging Practice Directions and Practice Forms and to the drafting team at the Lord Chancellor's Department for an early sight of a few proposed modifications to the published version of the Rules. I hope that as a result the text is as up-to-date as it is possible to be. My thanks are also due yet again to Mrs Christine McLean for typing the bulk of the manuscript and to the publishers for their customary support and encouragement. They will, I trust, note that the manuscript was on time — for once.

All errors are my responsibility.

David Foskett, Q.C.
March 19, 1999

CONTENTS

APPENDICES:

TABLE OF CASES

TABLE OF STATUTES

TABLE OF STATUTORY INSTRUMENTS

TABLE OF CIVIL PROCEDURE RULES

*Figures in **bold** type indicate where a Rule is set out in full.*

TABLE OF RULES OF THE SUPREME COURT

TABLE OF COUNTY COURT RULES

CHAPTER 1

The early settlement of disputes

The objective

One of the key objectives in the *Access to Justice* reforms is the promotion **1.1**
of the early settlement of disputes. In his Interim Report,[1] Lord Woolf said
that settlement "too often occurs at too late a stage in the proceedings,"[2]
the twin consequences being the expenditure of unnecessary costs and the
difficulties associated with listing cases that do require a trial. Of the
several working objectives put forward for the new system he envisaged,
one[3] was that whenever it is reasonable for the parties to do so, they
should settle their dispute before resorting to the courts, but that where
this was not achieved prior to the commencement of proceedings, they
should do so at as early a stage thereafter as possible. This working
objective was prominent in the new landscape for civil litigation envisaged
in Lord Woolf's Final Report[4] and, as already indicated, represents one of
the main aims of the reforms now being carried forward.

Achieving the objective

Setting an objective is one thing; achieving it is, of course, another. Since **1.2**
the settlement of a dispute created by two or more parties depends upon
the willingness of those same parties to make concessions, the question
arises of how those concessions can be encouraged legitimately by the very
system put in place to adjudicate on the disputes in the absence of
settlement. Generally speaking, a settlement will occur when each party to
a dispute has had a fair opportunity to appraise the strengths and

---

[1] *Access to Justice,* Interim Report, June 1995.
[2] *ibid.,* para. 37.
[3] *ibid.,* para. 7(b).
[4] *Access to Justice,* Final Report, July 1996, section 1, para. 9 and Chap. 10, para. 2, in
particular.

1

weaknesses of his own case and that of his opponent. Whilst opposing sides will still frequently arrive at differing perceptions of those strengths and weaknesses, the process often reveals an acceptable middle ground resulting in a compromise. A "fair opportunity" to appraise a case depends at least partly upon the availability of relevant information and documentation to each party. A system designed to encourage the early settlement of disputes will, as a basic minimum, require the earliest possible exchange of relevant information and documentation.

Pre-action protocols

1.3 In a number of areas of litigation, some of which[5] account for the largest number of civil cases instituted, pre-action protocols[6] are proposed. Lord Woolf has identified one of the purposes of such a code of practice as being "to enable [parties] to obtain the information they reasonably need in order to enter into an appropriate settlement."[7] In his Foreword to the first version of the "Pre-Action Protocol for the Resolution of Clinical Disputes"[8] the Lord Chancellor, Lord Irvine of Lairg, said this:

> "The protocol aims to improve the pre-action communication between the parties by establishing a timetable for the exchange of information relevant to the dispute and by setting standards for the content of correspondence. Compliance with the protocol will enable parties to make an informed judgment of the merits of their case earlier than tends to happen today, because they will have earlier access to the information they need. This will provide every opportunity for improved communication between the parties, designed to lead to an increase in the number of pre-action settlements."

1.4 There can be little doubt, it is submitted, that the existence of well-constructed pre-action protocols, supported by effective judicial sanctions in the event of non-compliance,[9] will be one of the greatest influences on

---

[5] e.g. personal injury litigation and litigation arising from alleged medical negligence.
[6] Defined in the Glossary to the Rules as "[s]tatements of understanding between legal practitioners and others about pre-action practice and which are approved by a relevant practice direction."
[7] Final Report, Chap. 10, para. 1.
[8] July 1998, in Modernising Justice (Cm. 4155), December 1998, pre-action protocols are identified as one of the main elements of the reform package: Chap. 4, para. 4.3.
[9] The need for effective judicial support for the observance of the protocols was emphasised by the Lord Chancellor in the Foreword referred to in n.8, above and in Modernising Justice. The extent to which a pre-action protocol has been complied with is a factor the court must take into account in deciding what, if any, order for costs to make (r.44.3(5)(a)) and which it will consider when deciding an application for relief from a sanction imposed for a failure to comply with any rule, practice direction or court order: r.3.9(1)(e). Rule 3.1(3)–(7) contains provisions enabling the court, in appropriate circumstances, to order a party to pay a sum of money into court if that party has, without good reason, failed to comply, inter alia, with "a relevant pre-action protocol".

the earlier settlement of the particular type of litigation to which they relate. In his Foreword to the Civil Procedure Rules, the Lord Chancellor emphasised that one of the tasks for the next phase of reform "is to increase the number of protocols so that the greatest number of cases fall within their scope."

Where no pre-action protocol

Merely because a pre-action protocol does not exist to cover a particular 1.5 piece of litigation will not, of course, preclude the court from penalising in costs a party whose conduct in not providing relevant information prior to commencement of proceedings has disabled the making of an informed pre-action offer[10] or an informed evaluation of a claimant's offer.[11]

The role of Alternative Dispute Resolution (ADR)

In the pre-action period the court is not in a position directly to influence 1.6 the conduct of the parties. It cannot, for example, encourage directly the use of some alternative means of resolving the dispute.[12] In his Final Report, Lord Woolf said[13] that the new procedures "would emphasise the importance of ADR through the court's ability to take into account whether parties have unreasonably rejected the possibility of ADR or have behaved unreasonably in the course of ADR." The draft costs rule put out for consultation contained a provision which entitled a court, in assessing the "conduct" of the parties, to take into account "whether they refused unreasonably to try an alternative dispute resolution procedure." However, the relevant part of the costs rule in the Civil Procedure Rules defining the "conduct" of the parties[14] does not contain a provision such as that appearing in the consultation draft. Indeed it makes no reference at all to ADR, although the non-exhaustive nature of the definition of conduct[15] would not, of course, preclude consideration of any relevant conduct including "conduct before . . . the proceedings". An unreasonable failure to agree to ADR could be subsumed within those general words.

---

[10] r.44.3(5) is wide enough to cover this.

[11] r.36.21(5)(d) draws attention specifically to the giving or refusing of information in the context of the court deciding what to do about costs when a *claimant's* Part 36 offer is bettered: see further at para. 11.17.

[12] Once proceedings are in existence, one of the specific case management powers referred to is the encouragement and facilitation of the use of an alternative dispute resolution procedure "if the court considers that appropriate": r.1.4(2)(e). See further at para. 1.11 *et seq.*, below.

[13] para. 18.

[14] r.44.3(5).

[15] "The conduct of the parties *includes* . . .": r.44.3(5). (Author's emphasis).

1.7 However, the stage has probably not yet been reached when the court is likely to penalise a party for not agreeing to ADR *per se*. This is, perhaps, reinforced by the White Paper *Modernising Justice*[16] in which the Lord Chancellor's Department indicates that the role of ADR is presently the subject of review. Paragraph 1.19 reads as follows:

> "The Government is also seeking to improve the range of options available to people for resolving disputes without a formal court adjudication process. There are several different models of 'alternative dispute resolution' (ADR), including mediation, arbitration and ombudsman schemes. We are considering what contribution these can make to a fair and effective civil justice system. ADR offers a number of possible advantages. It can be less formal and adversarial; and in some cases, it may allow disputes to be resolved more quickly and cheaply. Various ADR schemes already exist; and we have commissioned and published research into some of them, notably a court-based mediation scheme at the Central London County Court. We will be considering the evidence to see what benefits ADR can bring."

It is, therefore, likely that the courts will, at the very least, need to be better informed on an authoritative basis about the availability, efficacy and cost of ADR before being in a position to evaluate the reasonableness or otherwise of a refusal to engage in it.[17] The case management functions under the new rules will doubtless need to be exercised against the background of authoritative guidance on what role ADR can legitimately play in any orders or directions made.

1.8 Whilst that guidance can, perhaps, be regarded as "pending", there may be obvious cases where some alternative process to an adjudication by the court on an issue is more appropriate or would have been more appropriate. An example is afforded by the valuation of real or personal property. There is little point in a judge hearing evidence from two separate valuers and then effectively picking some suitable mid-point figure. A valuer appointed by *both* parties, or in default of agreement as to who it should be, by some independent third party (*e.g.* the President of the relevant institute), would seem to be the best person to resolve a dispute as to value. This approach has been used to good effect in the family finance jurisdiction for many years. It would be surprising if the court did not think it the only sensible, and cost effective, way of dealing with a disputed value in, say, either a boundary or partnership dispute.[18]

---

[16] n.8, above.

[17] The same proposition will also apply to any contemplated use of the court's case management powers under r.1.4(2)(e): n.12, above.

[18] *cf. Butcher v. Wolfe and Another, The Times*, November 9, 1998, CA.

As will be plain from the appraisal of the new rules that appears in the rest **1.9** of this work, the court's assessment of the parties' conduct in relation to settlement will be judged to a large extent on the basis of how an offer made and rejected compares with the ultimate decision of a court.[19] An unwillingness to respond constructively to a sensible pre-action offer admissible on the question of costs would almost certainly be treated by the court as one of "all the circumstances" to be taken into account on the issue of costs.[20] This is indeed already the case.[21] Until the role that ADR has or may have in facilitating a pre-action settlement is more clearly understood and accepted, it is unlikely to have a particularly significant impact on the court's decision as to the liability for costs.[22] It should, however, be noted that when the *assessment* of costs takes place, one of the factors to which the costs officer *must* have regard is "the efforts made, if any, before . . . the proceedings in order to try to resolve the dispute".[23] A suggestion for some kind of ADR might arguably constitute an effort to try to resolve the dispute. It would, however, be unlikely, save perhaps in exceptional circumstances, for the costs officer to penalise the party in costs for failing to respond positively to a suggestion for ADR if the court which dealt with the primary liability for costs made no adverse order or comment in this regard.

Agreement for ADR

If it be correct that the precise role of ADR in the pre-action period in the **1.10** context of the new rules remains undefined at the moment, there will, of course, be no impediment to the parties agreeing to ADR if they wish.[24] Commercial agreements quite frequently contain provisions for the deter- mination by experts of issues that may arise during the contract and these agreements are upheld by the courts.[25] For a number of years all divisions of the High Court have encouraged parties to focus on the possibility of resolving the whole or part of the dispute by ADR.[26] This kind of encouragement will have been reflected in local practice directions in regional specialist courts and various County Courts. Mediation is available in relation to appeals pending in the Court of Appeal.[27]

---

[19] See Chap. 11, in particular.
[20] r.44.3(4) and (5).
[21] *Butcher v. Wolfe and Another*, above; Foskett, *The Law of Practice and Compromise* (4th ed.), para. 9–06—9–10. *cf. Hobin v. Douglas, The Times*, December 29, 1998, CA.
[22] para. 1.7, above.
[23] r.44.5(3)(a)(ii).
[24] The Legal Aid Board's Costs Appeals Committee has decided that work carried out in advising on, preparing for and, where appropriate, attending a mediation hearing can in principle be allowable under Legal Aid in non-family cases: see *Focus*, December 1998.
[25] Foskett, *op cit.*, para. 4–50.
[26] *Practice Statement (Commercial Cases: Alternative Dispute Resolution)* [1994] 1 W.L.R. 14; *Practice Direction (Civil Litigation: Case Management)* [1995] 1 W.L.R. 508 at 510.
[27] *Practice Statement (Court of Appeal: Procedural Changes)* [1995] 1 W.L.R. 1189 at 1191.

Stay of proceedings to permit ADR

1.11 If parties are minded to try ADR, in general it would be desirable to embark upon it at an early stage in their dispute. The only *caveat* in respect of that general proposition is that any form of attempt at a resolution of the dispute, whether through ADR or simply through the efforts of the parties' representatives, will either be unproductive or potentially counter-productive if there has not been an appropriate degree of exchange of information and documentation before it takes place.[28] Suspicion will breed an unwillingness to negotiate and negotiation against the background of an inadequate exchange of information will be a fertile ground for dissatisfaction with the settlement achieved and thus for future litigation.

1.12 The message conveyed by the new rules is that even the commencement of proceedings is not too late to embark on ADR or other means of settlement. In the rules governing the preliminary stages of case management, provision is made for a stay "while the parties try to settle the case by alternative dispute resolution or other means."[29] This requires the agreement of "all parties" or the court can, of its own initiative, direct a stay if it considers that such a stay "would be appropriate."[30] The stay will be for "one month" in the first instance, but can be extended by the court (not the parties) "until such date or for such specified period as it considers appropriate."[31] The initial application for a stay for this purpose can be made by a letter to the court from one party which confirms that the application is made with the agreement of all parties. The letter must also explain the steps being taken and identify any mediator or expert assisting with the process.[32] Any party can apply to have the stay lifted[33] and the onus is on the claimant to inform the court if settlement is achieved.[34] If he does not inform the court by the end of the period of the stay that settlement has been achieved, the court will give appropriate case management directions.[35] Where a court order or court approval is required to effect any settlement achieved, the appropriate application will constitute an application for the stay to be lifted.[36]

---

[28] para. 1.2, above.
[29] r.26.4(1).
[30] r.26.4(2).
[31] *ibid.* and r.26.4(3). Any such extension "will generally be for no more than four weeks unless clear reasons are given to justify a longer time": Part 26 Practice Direction, para. 3.1(2)(b). More than one extension may be granted: *ibid.*, para. 3.1(3).
[32] Part 26 Practice Direction, para. 3.1(1)(b).
[33] *ibid.*, para. 3.3.
[34] r.26.4(4).
[35] r.26.4(5). See Part 26 Practice Direction, para. 3.2.
[36] Part 26 Practice Direction, para. 3.4.

Other incentives to settle

The manner in which other incentives to settle are provided for within the rules will be dealt with in due course.[37] Since the present discussion is primarily focused on the pre-action stage, it is important to note that the costs ordered to be paid by one party to another include "costs incurred *before* proceedings have begun".[38] Since considerably more pre-action activity than presently occurs is to be encouraged under the new system, it is only right that the costs arising in connection with a dispute should embrace appropriately incurred costs in that early stage. They will, of course, be subject to summary or detailed assessment by the court if they are not agreed. However, the significant point is that no party to a dispute can consider himself immune from paying his opponent's costs merely because they are being incurred during a period when no proceedings are on foot. Interest on those costs can be awarded.[39]

1.13

---

[37] Chap. 11.
[38] r.44.3(6)(d). (Author's emphasis).
[39] r.44.3(6)(g).

CHAPTER 2

The structure of Part 36

Introduction

2.1 Part 36 is where the detailed rules concerning offers to settle and payments into court are to be found. It replaces Order 22, Rules of the Supreme Court, and Order 11, County Court Rules, in relation to payments into court in respect of money claims and introduces provisions concerning offers to settle in respect of non-money claims. It provides also a machinery for making a combined offer to settle and a payment into court when the claim is for both monetary and non-monetary relief and the offeror wants to make a substantive offer in relation to each.

Not a complete code

2.2 Part 36 does not represent a complete code for determining the effect that an offer to settle or a payment into court may have upon the costs of the litigation to which it relates. First, whilst any party who wishes his offer to settle to be judged by reference to the provisions of Part 36 would be well advised to ensure that it is made precisely in accordance with those provisions, the court will not be precluded from giving effect to the normal consequences of Part 36 if it is not strictly in accordance with those provisions.[1] However, the court will only give effect to it in that way "if [it] so orders", whereas strict adherence to the terms of Part 36 will give rise automatically to the various consequences provided for in the provisions of Part 36.[2] Secondly, Part 36 says nothing about the costs consequences where a claimant (who has not himself made a claimant's

---

[1] r.36.1(2).
[2] r.36.1(1)(b). The Practice Direction says, at para. 1.3, that "[an] offer to settle which is not made in accordance with Part 36 will only have the consequences specified in that Part if the court so orders and will be given such weight on any issue as to costs as the court thinks appropriate."

Part 36 offer[3]) does better than the amount paid in, or the terms offered by, the defendant. Whilst the claimant in this situation will doubtless be regarded as the successful party and the defendant the "unsuccessful party", with the result that the latter will be ordered to pay the former's costs,[4] the costs rules require the court to consider the various matters set out in those rules before it exercises its discretion as to costs. There may be circumstances[5] which would dictate a different order from the general rule.

Freedom of contract

Just as Part 36 does not provide a complete code for determining the effect **2.3** of a payment into court or an offer to settle, neither does it prevent a party from making an offer in a way which avoids some or all of its provisions. Rule 36.1(2) makes it plain that the existence of Part 36 does not prevent a party making an offer to settle in whatever way he chooses. A pure "without prejudice" offer[6] would be outside Part 36 and would not, of course, be capable of being referred to on the question of the costs between the parties.[7] An open offer would, strictly speaking, be outside Part 36, although the offeror would probably wish to spell out that the intention is that it should have all the other consequences of Part 36.[8] Any offer made *orally* would not be within Part 36.[9] Any offer of a sum of money in a money claim would not be within Part 36.[10] A claimant's offer which expressly disavowed reliance on the provisions permitting the court to award higher interest if the court's award was better than the offer[11] would not be within Part 36.

It follows, therefore, that a party needs to "opt into" Part 36 in order to **2.4** guarantee that the court will treat the offer as one to which Part 36 applies. Where the claim is a money claim and a payment into court is made, there will be no doubt that the offeror intends Part 36 to apply. Where, however, an offer is made in respect of a non-money claim (*e.g.* a claim for a declaration in relation to a disputed boundary), the offeror would be well advised to state expressly that it is intended to be made in accordance with

---

[3] For claimants' offers, see, in particular, paras 2.3, 2.5, 3.3, 4.12, 10.11 and 11.9 *et seq.*
[4] r.44.3(2)(a).
[5] For example, a minimal improvement on a payment into court or offer to settle achieved at disproportionate expense: see Chap. 11.
[6] The intention of the Rules is to preserve the "without prejudice" privilege.
[7] *Cutts v. Head* [1984] Ch. 290, CA. It may still be possible to refer to a pure "without prejudice" offer on the issues that arise under section 17(1) of the Legal Aid Act 1988: see *McCallum v. Westridge Construction Company* [1971] C.L.Y. 9360.
[8] Precedent No. 6.
[9] r.36.5(1).
[10] Except where the offer is a pre-action offer by a defendant to a money claim which then becomes supported by a payment into court within 14 days of the service of the claim form on the claimant: r.36.10(3). See further in Chap. 3.
[11] r.36.21. See Chap. 11.

Part 36 if that is what he wishes.[12] However, even if this express statement is not made, but the manner in which the offer is phrased plainly brings it within Part 36, it is likely to be treated by the court as having been "made in accordance with this Part".[13] Furthermore, as already indicated,[14] the court can give effect to the consequences provided for in Part 36 even if the offer is not made "in accordance with" Part 36.

2.5 Little problem is likely to be presented in this regard in relation to an offer *made by a defendant* in a non-money claim provided, of course, the right to refer to the offer on the question of costs has been reserved. In that situation, if a claimant does not secure a decision from the court which is more advantageous than the offer, the almost inevitable consequence would be that he would have to pay the defendant's costs from the date when the offer expired. This is precisely the consequence provided for in relation to a Part 36 offer.[15] Where, however, a *claimant* makes a Part 36 offer (whether in relation to a money claim or a non-money claim), it might arguably be unjust for him to seek higher interest on any damages awarded (if greater than his offer), indemnity costs from the date when the offer could have been accepted and higher interest on those costs[16] unless he made it absolutely clear at the time of the offer that he would be relying upon Part 36.[17]

The privileged nature of offers within Part 36

2.6 A Part 36 offer will be treated as being "without prejudice except as to costs".[18] This means that whilst it can be referred to the court on the issue of costs,[19] it cannot be referred to on any other issue except in the very restricted circumstances that the law permits.[20] The purpose of retaining the "without prejudice" privilege is to enable negotiations to take place on a "cards on the table" basis without fear that anything said or done will be translated into some kind of admission.[21] The advantage to the offeror of being able to refer to the offer on the question of costs is that the offeree's conduct in rejecting it can be fully reflected in any order as to costs at the trial if the offer is not bettered.[22] Under existing practice, which will doubtless continue, offers of this nature may be referred to in appropriate circumstances during the pre-trial period.[23]

---

[12] Precedent No. 1. The Practice Direction (see Appendix I) states that a Part 36 offer "must . . . state that it is a Part 36 offer . . .": para.6.1.
[13] r.36.1(2).
[14] para. 2.2, above.
[15] r.36.20.
[16] r.36.21. See Chap. 11.
[17] Precedent No. 4.
[18] r.36.19(1).
[19] cf. *Calderbank v. Calderbank* [1976] Fam. 93; *Cutts v. Head*, above.
[20] Foskett, *op cit.*, para. 9–26 *et seq.*
[21] *ibid.*, para. 9–27 and 9–33.
[22] See Chap. 11.
[23] n.27, below.

With the exception of certain specific situations,[24] the general rule is that   2.7
the fact that a Part 36 payment has been made must not be communicated
to the trial judge "until all questions of liability and the amount of money
to be awarded have been decided".[25] The purpose of the rule is, of course,
to try to ensure that the trial judge is not influenced by knowledge of the
offer made. Since the rule refers specifically to the "trial Judge", the ability
exists, in appropriate circumstances, to draw the attention of the judge
exercising the pre-trial case management functions to the existence (and
indeed amount) of a Part 36 payment. Under existing practice, this can
occur in an application for an interim payment (once liability has been
admitted or established), an application for security for costs and in
response to an application to strike out for want of prosecution.[26] Evidence
of a Part 36 offer may be given during the pre-trial period in similar
circumstances.[27] This practice will undoubtedly continue.

The rule as to non-disclosure is expressed in mandatory terms[28] as is its   2.8
predecessor in the Rules of the Supreme Court.[29] Where, by inadvertence
or otherwise, that rule had been breached, the practice hitherto had been
for the trial judge to exercise a discretion as to whether to hear the case
further. Where satisfied that no injustice will be done, particularly if the
knowledge could be put to one side for the purpose of making his decision,
the trial judge could proceed.[30] Again, this practice is likely to continue. In
making any decision in this situation the trial judge will be obliged to try to
give effect to the overriding objective.[31] The overriding objective required
of the court is, so far as practicable, to save expense, to deal with a case
proportionately, expeditiously and fairly and to have regard to the need to
allot its resources to other cases.[32] In many cases those considerations
would reinforce the decision to proceed unless it was considered impracti-
cable to do so.

---

[24] para. 2.8, below.
[25] r.36.19(2).
[26] Foskett, *op cit.*, para. 9–47 *et seq.*
[27] *ibid.*
[28] "The fact that a Part 36 payment has been made *shall* not be communicated to the trial
Judge . . .": r.36.19(2). But see n.31 below.
[29] Ord. 22, r.7(1).
[30] *Millensted v. Grosvenor Place (Park Lane) Ltd* [1937] 1 K.B. 717, CA; *Re An Action for
Negligence* (1992 C. No. 3063), *The Times*, March 5, 1993, Knox J.
[31] r.1.2. It is, perhaps, debatable whether the power to continue to hear a case in the
circumstances referred to in the text is "given" to the court "by the rules": r.1.2(a). The
word "shall" in Ord. 22, r.7, Rules of the Supreme Court, was construed as "directory and
not compulsive": *Millensted v. Grosvenor House (Park Lane) Ltd*, above; *Gaskins v. British
Aluminium Company* [1976] Q.B. 524. That conclusion left room for a discretion to
proceed, the discretion being derived from the inherent jurisdiction of the court to control
its own proceedings: *per* Scott L.J. in *Millensted* at 725. It is unlikely that so refined an
analysis will be necessary under the new rules (which are to be interpreted so as to give
effect to the overriding objective: r.1.2(b)), but in so far as it may be necessary to look to
the inherent jurisdiction of the court for support, nothing in the rules is designed to prevent
recourse to that jurisdiction. It would, however, doubtless be exercised to give effect to the
overriding objective.
[32] r.1.1(2).

2.9 The existence of a Part 36 payment would be a relevant factor for the trial judge if the defence of tender before claim[33] was raised. Accordingly, in this situation the rule against disclosure of a Part 36 payment is expressly stated to be inapplicable.[34] Equally, there may be situations in which, once liability has been determined separately from the money claimed, the existence of the Part 36 payment may be relevant to the costs of the trial on liability. An express exemption from the general rule is provided for in this regard[35] so that the trial judge at the liability hearing can be told of the existence of the payment. Having been so told, one option available to the judge is to reserve the question of the costs of the liability issue to the trial of the assessment of the money claim. On the other hand, the absence of an offer at all on the question of liability, or the absence of an offer of a specified proportion (where, *e.g.* the issue of contributory negligence arises),[36] may result in the court granting the claimant the costs relating to that part of the proceedings.[37]

2.10 The third situation for which the rules provide an exception to the general rule is where the proceedings have been stayed "under r.36.15 following acceptance of a Part 36 offer or Part 36 payment".[38] By the time proceedings have been stayed under rule 36.15,[39] it would be extremely rare for a "trial judge" to become involved subsequently. Nonetheless, in such circumstances as may arise, reference to the payment into court may be made.

2.11 The existence of the rule against disclosure cannot, of course, prevent a party from applying to the trial judge for permission to accept a Part 36 payment in the circumstances where such an application may be entertained.[40] The previous rules were interpreted by the Court of Appeal in a way that required a plaintiff who wanted to accept a payment into court during a trial to obtain the consent of the defendant before making the application.[41] The view of the majority of the Court of Appeal was clearly influenced by a desire not to permit a plaintiff to try to gain a tactical advantage when a case was going badly by applying to take the payment into court, thus bringing it to the attention of the trial judge, and then seeking a re-trial before a different judge. However, the dissenting view drew attention to the lack of anything in the Rules which required the

---

[33] This is described in the Glossary to the Rules as being "[a] defence that, before the claimant started proceedings, the defendant unconditionally offered to the claimant the amount due or, if no specified amount is claimed, an amount sufficient to satisfy the claim."

[34] r.36.19(3)(a).

[35] r.36.19(3)(c).

[36] r.36.5(4).

[37] r.40.3(6)(f).

[38] r.36.19(3)(b).

[39] See para. 9.13 *et seq.*, below.

[40] r.36.11(2)(a) and (b)(ii).

[41] *Gaskins v. British Aluminium* Co. above, *per* Lord Denning M.R. and Orr L.J. Browne L.J. dissented on the point, taking the view that a plaintiff could apply during the trial to take out a payment into court "whether or not the defendant consents".

defendant's consent to such an application and to the existence of the discretion of the court to continue with the trial notwithstanding the judicial knowledge thus gained.[42] So far as the new rules are concerned, it is submitted that there is nothing that requires the consent of the defendant before a claimant may make such an application during a trial. Attention has already been drawn to the likely response of the court if a claimant then sought a trial before a different judge.[43]

---

[42] para. 2.8, above.
[43] *ibid.*

CHAPTER 3

Pre-action offers

Background

3.1 Under the previous rules, an offer to settle a case, whether involving a money claim or a non-money claim, achieved a status recognised by the rules only when proceedings were in existence. A payment into court could be made only when "an action for a debt or damages"[1] was in existence. A written offer made "without prejudice save as to costs" was, if made pursuant to the rules, only capable of being made by "[a] party to the proceedings" in relation "to any issue in the proceedings".[2] An offer of settlement "up to a specified proportion" on the issue of liability achieved a status under the rules only after an order for a split trial had been made.[3] An offer of contribution by a third party achieved recognition only after the third party became "a party to an action".[4] The rules did oblige the court to take into account offers of settlement of the nature mentioned above "in exercising his discretion as to costs",[5] but did not oblige him to take account of any pre-litigation offer.[6]

3.2 Consistent with the policy of encouraging earlier settlement,[7] the new rules give added status to a pre-action offer. If any such offer is translated into a settlement, then that, of course, ends the dispute. If, notwithstanding the offer, proceedings are instituted, rule 36.10(1) provides that "the court

---

[1] RSC, Ord. 22, r.1(1).
[2] RSC, Ord. 22, r.14(1).
[3] RSC, Ord. 33, r.4A.
[4] RSC, Ord. 16, r.10.
[5] RSC, Ord. 62, r.9(1).
[6] Notwithstanding the phraseology of the old rules, the practice was for the court to take account of an offer of settlement, certainly in a non-money claim, made before proceedings were issued: *cf. Snuggs v. Seyd and Kelly's Credit Index Co.* [1894] W.N. 95; *Butcher v. Wolfe and Anor, The Times,* November 9, 1998, CA.
[7] Chap. 1.

will take that offer into account when making any order as to costs",[8] provided that the offer "complies with the provisions of this rule". How does the offeror comply with the provisions of the rule?

The offer itself

For the pre-action offer to achieve a status within the rules it must—   3.3

    (a) be kept open "for at least 21 days after the date it was made";
    (b) if made by someone who would be a defendant to any proceedings commenced, "include an offer to pay the costs of the offeree incurred up to the date 21 days after the date it was made".[9]

It must also "otherwise comply with" Part 36.[10] In other words, it must contain the details required by Part 36.[11]

An offer under this rule is "made" when it is received by the offeree,[12] as   3.4 indeed is a Part 36 offer made after proceedings have begun.[13] Although the formal provision within the rules enabling an offeree to seek clarification of a Part 36 offer or payment notice[14] does not strictly apply to a pre-action offer, any failure to give clarification where it would have been a reasonable course to take is likely to be "conduct" that the court could take into account in relation to costs.[15]

As with any contractual offer, a pre-action offer may be withdrawn (or   3.5 revoked) at any time before its acceptance.[16] It may be withdrawn before the time given for acceptance has run its course.[17] Once the specified period for acceptance has expired, it cannot thereafter be accepted.[18]

---

[8] This provision can, perhaps, be seen merely as a statement reflecting the mandatory obligation on the court to have regard to "any admissible offer to settle made by a party which is drawn to the court's attention (whether or not made in accordance with Part 36)": r.44.3(4)(c).

[9] r.36.10(2)(a) and (b). A claimant's pre-action offer may say nothing about costs. If that is so and it is accepted, the natural consequence would be that each party would bear his own costs: Foskett, *op cit.*, para. 5–21. Alternatively, a claimant may invite the party who would be a defendant to agree to pay the claimant's costs either to the date of the offer, to the date of acceptance or to a date 21 days after the offer: see Precedent No. 4.

[10] r.36.10(2)(c).

[11] See Chap. 5.

[12] r.36.10(5).

[13] r.36.8(1).

[14] r.36.9. See Chap. 8, below.

[15] See para. 1.8, above. *cf. Butcher v. Wolfe and Anor, The Times,* November 9, 1998, CA.

[16] *Chitty on Contracts,* (27th ed.), para. 2–059 *et seq.*

[17] *ibid.*

[18] *ibid.,* para. 2–066. An offer can, of course, be renewed after the expiration of such a period, but it effectively becomes a new offer.

3.6 A pre-action offer that is withdrawn is unlikely to have any significant impact on the question of costs at the end of a trial.[19] One which is refused or not accepted is, of course, in a different category. If the offeree ultimately succeeds in merely matching the offer, or achieves less, then the costs expended after refusing or not accepting the offer will have been wasted.

3.7 What happens if the offeree changes his mind subsequently and decides that he would like to accept the offer? As already indicated,[20] the offer will have lapsed and will not be available for acceptance. In this situation, the offeree needs to become an offeror in his own right. In terms which are appropriate to the particular dispute, he will need to state that he offers to settle the case on the terms previously offered by the original offeror, perhaps offering to pay the original offeror's costs arising after the period for acceptance had expired. Provided that the offer complies with the requirements of Part 36,[21] it would become a pre-action offer in its own right capable of being considered on the question of costs.

3.8 The process described in the preceding paragraph shows that there could be a number of unaccepted pre-action offers for the court to consider at the end of a trial. With the emphasis being placed on pre-litigation negotiations, this should not be regarded as an unwelcome scenario. Plainly, though, the resolution of the issue of costs could be somewhat complex.

Further requirements — money claims

3.9 Where the offeror is potentially a defendant in proceedings in which money is to be claimed, he must make a Part 36 payment[22] "within 14 days of service of the claim form" in a sum which "must not be less than the sum offered before proceedings began".[23]

3.10 The proviso concerning the amount paid into court is important. Plainly, a Part 36 payment in a sum *less* than the amount previously offered could not be referable to, or relate back to, the pre-action offer. Equally, a Part 36 payment in a sum *greater* than the amount of the pre-action offer could

---

[19] It would be difficult to say that such an offer was an wholly irrelevant factor given the wide ambit of the court's discretion on costs, but it is difficult to see how it could have any appreciable influence on the court's decision. In his Final Report, Lord Woolf said that "obviously the court would not take account of a withdrawn offer when considering costs except when considering the reasonableness of the parties' conduct generally." (Chap.11, para.5).

[20] para. 3.5, above.

[21] n.11, above.

[22] See Chap. 6. The form of the Part 36 payment notice will have to be modified to show that the payment is made in support of a pre-action offer: see Precedent No. 11.

[23] r.36.10(3).

be seen as not relating to that offer: the recipient of the Part 36 payment notice in respect of a sum greater than the pre-action offer could quite reasonably interpret the payment into court as being a *new* offer of settlement. He might elect to accept it within 21 days on the usual terms as to costs.[24] As indicated below,[25] a Part 36 payment made under this rule may not be accepted without the permission of the court. It would seem, therefore, that an offeror of a sum of money who wishes in subsequent proceedings to stand on his pre-action offer should pay into court a sum *equal* to that offer. It would not be necessary to add further interest to that sum in respect of the period between the offer and the date of the Part 36 payment because the offer is to be judged by reference to the time it was made, not by reference to the time of the subsequent payment into court.

Further requirements — non-money claims

Unlike a money claim,[26] where a pre-action offer has been made in a non-money claim, the rules do not require any step to be taken by the offeror in relation to that offer at or about the time that the proceedings begin. The need for a payment into court in furtherance of a pre-action offer in a money claim reflects the policy of requiring the offeror to demonstrate his financial standing and of ensuring the existence of an inducement to the offeree to accept in the sense of knowing that "the money is there". The payment in is made at the first opportunity there is to make one after the commencement of proceedings. No equivalent policy can operate in relation to a non-money claim and, accordingly, there is nothing further to be done once proceedings are on foot. **3.11**

Can a pre-action offer be accepted after proceedings have started?

Given the legal effect of an unaccepted pre-action offer,[27] the answer to the question posed may seem obvious: it cannot be accepted. However, the reason for posing the question is that rule 36.10(4) at first sight appears to contemplate the possibility of acceptance "after proceedings have begun", albeit not "without the permission of the court." How can the court give permission to the offeree to accept an offer (possibly made many months, or even years, previously) which is no longer open for acceptance? Can the rules have the effect of breathing new life into an offer that has expired? If so, is it right that the person who rejected the offer previously should be able to secure this by the unilateral step of commencing proceedings? **3.12**

---

[24] See para. 9.4 *et seq.*
[25] para. 3.12, above.
[26] paras 3.9 and 3.10, above.
[27] para. 3.5, above.

3.13 Phrased in the way that they were, the foregoing questions would each attract an essentially negative answer. On the other hand, in the case-managed system of civil justice there is at least an argument that a previously *unwithdrawn* offer is something of which the court, if it is asked to do so after the expiry of the offer, should be able to permit acceptance, albeit only upon terms which ensure justice for the offeror. The court would presumably not entertain sympathetically any such application if the offeree's prospects in the dispute had altered adversely compared with his prospects at the time of the offer. Equally, the court would need to ensure that the offeror was not out of pocket in relation to his costs. These are essentially the conditions that applied under the previous rules relating to the acceptance of a payment into court after the normal time for acceptance had expired.[28] Indeed, under those rules the court did control the terms upon which the money in court might be accepted by the offeree after the normal period for acceptance[29] or be withdrawn by the offeror either before or after that period for acceptance had expired.[30]

3.14 It would appear that, in relation to money claims, the new rules will permit the court to entertain an application for acceptance of the money paid into court in furtherance of a pre-action offer even though the offer had not been accepted when made originally.[31] In a practical sense, the ability to do so is facilitated by the requirement that money should be paid into court by the offeror if he wishes his pre-action offer to be considered within the rules. Before making that payment into court the offeror will, of course, have made a conscious decision about the matter. The rule which enables the court to entertain such an application is expressed in precisely the same way in relation to pre-action offers in non-money claim cases.[32] Although at first sight this might suggest that a similar jurisdiction exists in relation to such cases, the intention underlying the rules was not to interfere with the freedom of a party to withdraw his offer at any time.[33] It is suggested, therefore, that a previously unaccepted pre-action offer cannot be the subject of an application to the court by the offeree for permission to accept once proceedings are on foot.

3.15 In some cases an offeror in a non-money claim (*e.g.* in claims for a declaration about a boundary) may wish to put his pre-action offer on effectively the same footing as a pre-action offer in a money claim which crystallises formally on the making of the requisite payment into court

---

[28] *Gaskins v. British Aluminium Co.* [1976] Q.B. 524, CA; *Garner v. Cleggs* [1983] 1 W.L.R. 862, CA; *Black v. Doncaster Metropolitan Borough Council* [1999] 1 W.L.R. 53, CA.
[29] *ibid. Proetta v. Times Newspapers Ltd* [1991] 1 W.L.R. 337, CA.
[30] *Metroinvest Ansalt v. Commercial Union Assurance Co.* [1985] 1 W.L.R. 513, CA; *Manku v. Seehra* (1987) 7 Con.L.R. 90. Foskett, *op cit.*, para.10–07.
[31] r.36.10(4).
[32] *ibid.*
[33] See para. 3.5, above. See also para. 2.3, above, and paras 5.3–5.4, below. The express reference in r.36.5(8) to the fact that a "withdrawn" Part 36 offer is not to have the consequences set out in Part 36 evidences the intention that an offeror should be able to withdraw an offer if he wishes to do so.

shortly after the commencement of the proceedings.[34] It is suggested that there are two ways of achieving this:

(i) by writing a suitable letter[35] within 14 days of the commencement of proceedings confirming the continued availability for acceptance of the offer "with the court's permission";

(ii) by so phrasing the pre-action offer when it is made to make it clear that it will continue to be open for acceptance after it expires (including after the commencement of proceedings) albeit upon altered terms as to costs.[36] This approach is not infrequently adopted when making sealed offers in arbitration proceedings.

---

[34] paras 3.9 and 3.10, above.
[35] Precedent No. 9.
[36] Precedent No. 8.

CHAPTER 4

The essential general requirements of a Part 36 offer and a Part 36 payment notice

Introduction

4.1 This Chapter deals with those requirements of the rules which are common (or effectively common) both to Part 36 offers as such and Part 36 payment notices. Chapter 5 deals with the additional specific requirements relating to a Part 36 offer, Chapter 6 deals with those relating to a Part 36 payment notice and Chapter 7 with those relating to offers of settlement in mixed claims.

Form

4.2 A Part 36 offer must be in writing.[1] A Part 36 payment notice[2] is, of course, a document.

The matters to which either can relate

4.3 A Part 36 offer and a Part 36 payment notice "may relate to the whole claim or to part of it or to any issue that arises in it"[3] and each must state whether "it relates to the whole of the claim or to part of it or to an issue that arises in it and if so to which part or issue".[4]

---

[1] r.36.5(1).
[2] r.36.6(2).
[3] r.36.5(2) and 36.6(1).
[4] rr.36.5(3)(a) and 36.6(2)(b).

"The whole of the claim"

The natural meaning of this expression connotes all issues that arise **4.4** directly in the proceedings. It will probably also include all the issues that arise indirectly in the proceedings as well as those which could have been raised, but were not raised specifically.[5]

In most cases, the "whole of the claim" will embrace primary liability, **4.5** contributory negligence (where applicable), causation of loss and all issues relating to the remoteness and quantification of damages. Where relief in the form of an injunction or other equitable remedy is sought, it will include that relief as well.

Interest

Under the old rules, interest was deemed to be included in the plaintiff's **4.6** cause of action in respect of a debt or for damages for the purposes of a payment into court.[6] The effect of the new rules is also to make any offer to settle a money claim to be *inclusive* of interest unless the contrary is expressed. Any Part 36 offer and any Part 36 payment is required to give certain details in relation to interest "if it is expressed not to be inclusive of interest".[7] The details required in that event (and the details required in any non-inclusive claimant's Part 36 offer to accept a sum of money[8]) are—

(a) whether interest *is* offered; and
(b) if it is, the amount offered, the rate or rates offered and the period or periods for which it is offered.[9]

Parts and issues

The resolution of discrete issues represents one of the objectives of the **4.7** "active case management" required by the new rules.[10] Encouraging parties to focus on the real issues in dispute will ensure a more efficient and economic disposal of the case. Although, in practice, many issues were resolved in proceedings governed by the old rules, the rules themselves, particularly those relating to payments into court, were largely framed to

---

[5] *i.e.* the kind of issues that would now be treated as *res judicata* in the wider sense of the *Henderson v. Henderson* principle.
[6] RSC, Ord. 22, r.1(8).
[7] rr.36.5(3)(c) and 36.6(2)(e).
[8] r.36.22.
[9] r.36.22(2). See Precedent Nos 7, 10 and 11.
[10] r.1.4(2)(b), (d) and (f).

facilitate the settlement of either the whole case or to particular "causes of action" within it.[11] After 1986, the rules permitted the making of a written offer to any other party to the proceedings (expressed to be "without prejudice save as to costs") in relation to "any issue in the proceedings"[12] and the court was obliged to take any such offer into account on the questions of costs unless, at the time it was made, the party making it "could have protected his position as to costs by means of a payment into court".[13] Framing the offer correctly was often of great importance.[14]

4.8 The phraseology of the new rules paves the way, for example, for the making of a payment into court by a defendant in a substantial personal injuries claim against a particular part of the claim. A significant feature of many such claims is the cost of future care for a severely disabled claimant. This could clearly be interpreted as "part" of the overall money claim or as an "issue" within it such that a Part 36 payment in relation to it could be made.[15]

4.9 How this greater flexibility within the rules is utilised by parties and encouraged by the courts will only become apparent as the change to a case-managed system develops. The plainly desirable objective of encouraging parties to resolve as many issues as they can will have to be balanced against the possibly undesirable fragmentation of an overall claim to the point where its true nature is no longer discernible. The prospect of a claimant facing, say, six different payments into court against six specific heads of claim, with another six having no offers made in respect of them, is not something, it is thought, that the courts would generally wish to encourage. Furthermore, in cases where the courts' approval to the acceptance of a payment into court is required,[16] the giving of such approval is not always easy unless the overall picture is available for consideration. At all events, the way in which this particular part of the new rules is applied in practice will be very much a reflection of how case management techniques are themselves applied having regard to the overriding objective of the rules.[17]

Liability up to a specified proportion

4.10 A defendant can make a Part 36 offer limited to accepting liability up to a specified proportion.[18]

---

[11] RSC, Ord. 22, rr.1–3. See, *e.g.*, *Toprak Enerji Sanayi A.S. v. Sale Tilney Plc* [1994] 1 W.L.R. 840.
[12] RSC, Ord. 22, r.14(1).
[13] RSC, Ord. 62, r.9(1)(d).
[14] *Hobin v. Douglas, The Times,* December 29, 1998, CA.
[15] For the consequences of acceptance, see Chap. 9.
[16] See Chap. 10.
[17] r.1.1.
[18] r.36.5(4).

Counterclaims

Where the party responding to a claim (either in the pre- or post-litigation **4.11** stage) intimates a counterclaim, he must, if making a Part 36 offer or a Part 36 payment, "state whether it takes into account [the] counterclaim".[19] Since a Part 36 offer may be made by a claimant, the same rule as applies to a defendant's Part 36 offer will also apply to such an offer. Since Part 36 applies to all parties who are or might become involved in an action,[20] the need to specify whether an offer takes account of "any"[21] counterclaim may be important if any such claim has been intimated or commenced by or against any such party. Any failure to do so could almost certainly entitle the offeree to seek and obtain clarification of the offer or Part 36 payment notice.[22]

Interim payments

A Part 36 offer can be made by reference to an interim payment.[23] **4.12** Furthermore, where a Part 36 payment is made in respect of a money claim, the notice must state whether any interim payment already made has been taken into account.[24] Although this is the only provision in Part 36 that requires an offer to settle to make specific reference to a prior interim payment, it would be advisable for a reference to the same effect to be made in any pre-action offer, whether by a claimant or a likely defendant, and in any claimant's Part 36 offer made after proceedings have begun. A possible consequence of not doing so is that the offer will be treated as excluding the interim payment and any consequent settlement may be in a higher sum than the offeror truly intended. An "interim payment" is, by definition, a payment "on account of any damages, debt or other sum (except costs) which the court may hold the defendant liable to pay".[25] These words suggest that any interim payment is to be regarded as part of the final sum awarded. However, without expressly so stating when an offer of settlement is made, it would be possible to interpret the offer as "£X plus the interim payment" rather than "£X inclusive of the interim payment".

---

[19] rr.36.5(3)(b) and 36.6(2)(c).
[20] *i.e.* those making a "Part 20 claim": r.20.2.
[21] n.19, above.
[22] r.36.9. See Chap. 8.
[23] r.36.5(5).
[24] r.36.6(2)(d).
[25] r.25.1(1)(k).

CHAPTER 5

Particular requirements of a Part 36 offer

Definition

5.1 A "Part 36 offer" for this purpose is one which is made *after* proceedings have started[1] and relates solely to a non-money claim.[2] A pre-action offer in a non-money claim achieves a status within Part 36 only when proceedings have begun.[3] That status, however, is not equivalent to the status of a true Part 36 offer: it is merely that of being available for consideration by the court on the question of costs at the conclusion of the trial.[4]

Time given for acceptance

5.2 An offer made *more than 21 days before the start of the trial* will not fall within the provisions of Part 36 if it fails to state expressly that it remains "open for acceptance for 21 days from the date it is made".[5] (A Part 36 offer is "made" when it is "received by the offeree".)[6] It must also provide that after 21 days the offeree may accept it only if either "the parties agree the liability for costs" or "the court gives permission".[7] Those latter requirements are also mandatory in relation to an offer made "*less* than 21 days before the start of the trial".[8]

---

[1] r.36.2(4)(a).
[2] An offer to settle a money claim must be made by way of a payment into court called a "Part 36 payment": see Chap. 6.
[3] Chap. 3.
[4] r.36.10(1).
[5] r.36.5(6)(a). See Precedent Nos 1, 3, 4 and 5.
[6] r.36.8(1).
[7] r.36.5(6)(b). See para. 5.7, below.
[8] r.36.5(7). For the kind of considerations arising in relation to costs at this stage, see para. 10.6 *et seq.*

The rules recognise that any offer of this nature is a contractual offer and 5.3
subject to the normal legal principles applicable to such an offer.[9] One
option available to an offeror is the withdrawal of the offer before the time
given for acceptance has expired. The rules provide that if a Part 36 offer is
withdrawn "it will not have the consequences set out in this part".[10]

Consistent with the normal principles of the law of contract, a Part 36 5.4
offer may be withdrawn not merely within any period of 21 days or more
granted for acceptance, but also at any time before the court gives
permission for it to be accepted after that period of 21 days or more has
expired.[11] Unlike a Part 36 payment, which can be withdrawn only with
the court's permission,[12] a Part 36 offer can be withdrawn at any time.[13]

Since a withdrawn Part 36 offer is unlikely to have any, or any significant, 5.5
impact on the question of costs, it will probably be only in the rarest of
circumstances that an offeror will elect to withdraw the offer. In a
boundary dispute, the discovery of a previously unknown map, plan or
statutory declaration which significantly altered the balance of the argument about the location of the disputed boundary affords an obvious
example of the situation in which an offeror might wish to withdraw the
offer. It would, if the matter ever got that far, give the court grounds for
declining the grant of permission to the offeree to accept the offer after its
period for acceptance had expired.[14]

Alteration of Part 36 offer

Where a Part 36 offer is altered, it constitutes a new offer. The rules 5.6
provide that an "improvement to a Part 36 offer will be effective when its

---

[9] para. 3.5, above.
[10] r.36.5(8).
[11] r.36.5(6)(b)(ii) requires the offeror to stipulate that the offer may be accepted after that
period if the court gives permission. It remains to be seen whether a court would feel
obliged to recognise the right of the offeror to withdraw the offer right up to the time it is
about to give its ruling on an application by the offeree to accept it. That would seem to be
the strict contractual position. However, it would be very unattractive to sanction a course
which entitled the offeror to contest on its merits an application by the offeree for
permission to accept the offer late, but then to withdraw it if it appeared to him that the
decision of the court was going to be adverse.
[12] See para. 6.11.
[13] A proposal that the rules should provide that a Part 36 offer could not be withdrawn
without the permission of the court was twice considered and twice rejected by the Civil
Procedure Rule Committee. Two views were expressed: one was that to provide in this way
would offend the normal contractual principles referred to in the text; the other was that
the choice of "opting into" Part 36 (with the consequent inability to withdraw the offer
without the permission of the court) would be entirely the offeror's and that, having made
that choice, the normal contractual principles would be offended no more than they are by
the rules relating to payments into court. The former view prevailed.
[14] See n.28 in Chap. 3.

details are received by the offeree".[15] Consistent with the need for a Part 36 offer to be in writing,[16] it is likely that the "details" of any improved offer will need to have been reduced to writing.

The court's permission to accept a Part 36 offer

5.7 The factors which the court will regard as relevant to the grant or refusal of permission to accept a Part 36 offer after the time for acceptance has expired are likely to be the same as, or similar to, those applicable in relation to an application to accept a Part 36 payment "out of time". Those factors will be reviewed later.[17]

---

[15] r.36.8(3).
[16] para. 4.2, above.
[17] See Chap. 10.

CHAPTER 6

Particular requirements of a Part 36 payment and a Part 36 payment notice

Definition of Part 36 payment

A "Part 36 payment" is the payment of a sum of money into court after **6.1** proceedings have commenced in pursuance of an offer to settle a money claim.[1] Consistent with the policy to which reference has already been made,[2] an offeror will not be able to rely upon the provisions of Part 36 in respect of a money claim unless he makes a Part 36 payment. Two exceptions to this rule are expressly provided for by rule 36.3(1).[3] Subject to those exceptions, an offer by a defendant to a money claim to settle that claim "will not have the consequences set out in [Part 36] unless it is made by way of a Part 36 payment."[4]

Part 36 payment notice

The requirements of a Part 36 offer and a Part 36 payment that are **6.2** common to each other have already been reviewed.[5] These relate essentially to the matters in respect of which the offer to settle is made. Does it, for example, relate to the whole or part of a claim, or simply to an issue or issues, and if so what part or what issue or issues? When a Part 36 offer is

---

[1] r.36.2(1) and (4); r.36.3.
[2] para. 3.11, above.
[3] The first is where an offer to settle is made "by reference to an interim payment" within r.36.2(3). The second is where the offeror has applied for, but has not yet received, a certificate of recoverable benefit from the Compensation Recovery Unit at the time he makes his offer, provided that he *does* make a Part 36 payment within seven days of receiving the certificate: r.36.23(2).
[4] r.36.3(1).
[5] Chap. 4, above.

made, these matters will be identified in the offer itself; when a Part 36 payment is made, they must be identified on the Part 36 payment notice.[6]

6.3 Neither the rules nor the Practice Direction stipulate that a Part 36 payment notice must be in a prescribed practice form. However, an offeror would be well advised to adopt the standard form or to model his own upon it to ensure that the relevant information appears on the face of the notice.[7]

The mechanics of payment

6.4 The payment is made usually by way of a cheque, either in favour of the Accountant General of the Supreme Court if the proceedings are in the Royal Courts of Justice, or to Her Majesty's Paymaster General when the proceedings are elsewhere.[8]

The mechanics of service of the notice

6.5 When a Part 36 payment is made, the Part 36 payment notice must be filed with the court.[9] Unless the offeree informs the court at the time he makes the payment into court that he will serve the notice himself, the court will serve the Part 36 payment notice.[10] Where the offeror is concerned to ensure the earliest possible service of the notice, he may well choose to serve it himself. This has been the required practice in the High Court hitherto and a practice frequently followed by solicitors in the county court. Under the new rules, when the court effects service of a document, it may decide which of the various available methods of service[11] is to be used.[12] Where the offeror regards time as of the essence, he may, for example, wish to give notice by means of fax or other means of electronic communication.[13] Electing to serve a Part 36 notice himself may give him greater control over the process. Where he does elect to serve the Part 36 payment notice he must, after doing so, file a certificate of service.[14] The rules refer to the service of "*the* Part 36 payment notice". It would seem to follow that, so far as practicable, the original should be used for the purposes of service, the court doubtless retaining some form of copy for its

---

[6] r.36.6(2).
[7] Precedent No. 11.
[8] Part 36 Practice Direction, para. 5.
[9] r.36.6(2).
[10] r.36.6(3).
[11] r.6.3(2).
[12] r.6.2(1).
[13] r.6.2(1)(e) and the relevant Practice Direction.
[14] rr.36.6(4) and 6.10.

records. The important objective, however, is to ensure that the offeree receives, at a time capable of identification, "written notice"[15] of the payment into court, including, of course, the terms upon which the payment is made. From the moment that information is conveyed in the required form to him, the period for acceptance[16] starts running.

Increased payment into court

Where the offeror decides to increase the amount of his Part 36 payment, 6.6 that further sum must be paid into court in accordance with the practice identified above and a new Part 36 payment notice must be served. The increase in the Part 36 payment will take effect "when notice of the increase is served on the offeree".[17]

The 21-day rule

As already noted, a Part 36 offer made more than 21 days before the start 6.7 of the trial must give the offeree 21 days from the date it is received by him to accept it. A Part 36 offer made less than 21 days before the start of the trial may only be accepted without the permission of the court if the parties agree the liability for costs.[18] The same effect is given by the rules to a Part 36 payment.

Unless sufficient circumstances exist to warrant the court giving permission 6.8 for the withdrawal of a Part 36 payment,[19] any such payment made not less than 21 days before the trial is capable of acceptance by the offeree within 21 days of it being made without the need for the court's permission.[20] A Part 36 payment made less than 21 days before the trial may not be accepted without the permission of the court unless the parties agree the liability for costs.[21]

Unlike the position under the old rules, the *only* circumstance in which a 6.9 payment into court can be accepted with the automatic costs consequences[22] is acceptance within 21 days of a payment into court made not less than 21 days before the trial.[23] In every other situation, as indicated

---

[15] r.36.8(2).
[16] See Chap. 9.
[17] r.36.8(4).
[18] para. 5.2, above.
[19] See para. 6.11.
[20] r.36.11(1).
[21] r.36.11(2).
[22] See Chap. 9.
[23] Under the old rules, the plaintiff had the right to accept a payment into court made before the trial whenever it was made provided it was accepted (a) within 21 days of the notice of payment into court having been received and (b) provided the trial or hearing had not begun: Ord.22, r.3(1). This interpretation was the interpretation assumed by the Court of Appeal in *King v. Weston-Howell* [1989] 1 W.L.R. 579 at 584. Equally, any payment into court made for the first time after the trial had begun, or any increase during the trial of a payment into court made before the trial had begun, could be accepted within two days without the leave of the court.

above, the permission of the court is required unless the parties agree the liability for costs.[24]

The effectiveness of a Part 36 payment outside the 21-day rule

6.10 The fact that a Part 36 payment is made within 21 days of the trial will not necessarily disqualify it from consideration on the question of costs.[25] There is a positive obligation on the court to have regard to any "payment into court" when considering its order as to costs[26] and it should be recalled that a Part 36 payment (and indeed a Part 36 offer) "may be made *at any time* after proceedings have started".[27]

The withdrawal of a Part 36 payment

6.11 A Part 36 payment may be withdrawn only with the permission of the court.[28] The circumstances in which, under the former rules, leave to withdraw a payment into court might be given have been stated previously.[29] The guiding factor was the change, if any, in the plaintiff's prospects in the action between the date of the payment in and the date of the application for withdrawal. It is likely, it is thought, that this will still remain a central factor in the court's approach to any such application under the new rules. However, given the nature of case management and the obligation on the parties to help further the overriding objective,[30] it is possible that the court would entertain such an application on wider grounds. If, for example, a claimant failed to give proper disclosure of documents in support of his claim, that may afford grounds for concluding that it would be unfair to hold a defendant to a particular Part 36 payment. Again, this is an area in which a practice will doubtless develop as the case-managed system becomes established.

---

[24] The rationale for this is that in a case-managed system of civil justice, with the early exchange of relevant information and documentation, there should be no reason why an appropriate Part 36 payment (or, in non-money cases, an appropriate Part 36 offer) should not be made at least 21 days before the trial.

[25] This was also the position under the old rules: see *King v. Weston-Howell*, above.

[26] r.44.3(4)(c).

[27] r.36.2(4)(a). (Emphasis added.)

[28] r.36.6(5).

[29] para. 3.13 and the cases referred to in n.29 in Chap. 3.

[30] r.1.3.

CHAPTER 7

Mixed money and non-money claims

The old rules

Under the former rules, a payment into court could be made only in an 7.1 "action for a debt or damages" in satisfaction of "the cause of action in respect of which the plaintiff claims".[1] Acceptance of the payment into court would result in the automatic stay of "all further proceedings . . . in respect of the specified cause of action".[2] This was seen as preventing a plaintiff from keeping open, say, a claim for an injunction arising out of a cause of action in respect of which he was prepared to accept the sum in court in satisfaction of the damages claim.[3] This made the decision as to acceptance of a payment into court in this kind of situation difficult. Equally, a defendant could be placed in difficulty in making an offer of settlement effective on the question of costs.[4]

The new rules

The phraseology of the present rules allows for greater flexibility in 7.2 relation to making a Part 36 payment. Where a defendant to what is solely a money claim wants to offer money in settlement, he must pay that sum of

---

[1] RSC, Ord. 22, r.1. A claim for an account of profits was not a claim for debt or damages: *Braben v. Emap Images Ltd* [1997] 1 W.L.R. 1507. See also *Malhotra v. Dhawan* [1997] 8 Med. L.R. 319, CA.

[2] RSC, Ord. 22, r.3(4).

[3] *Hargreaves Construction (Lineside) Ltd v. Williams and Anor, The Times,* July 3, 1982, Foster J. The counter-argument to this view is that the payment into court could *only* be made against the claim for damages and thus could not prevent the claim for the other relief from proceeding: *cf. Young v. Black Sluice Commissioners* (1903) 73 J.P. 265.

[4] Foskett, *op cit.,* para. 9–15.

money into court.[5] However, if he is faced solely with a claim for an injunction (so that there is no claim for money), there is nothing to prevent him from making a Part 36 payment in respect of that claim if he wishes. If the court eventually awards damages in lieu of an injunction there would be no reason in principle why the payment into court should not be fully effective on the question of costs. Equally, if a defendant is faced with a money claim and a non-money claim, and is prepared to settle one and argue against the other on the merits, he can either make a Part 36 payment in respect of part of the case (or an issue within it),[6] or make no Part 36 payment but make a Part 36 offer in relation to the non-money claim. Provided that the Part 36 payment notice or the Part 36 offer is sufficiently clear,[7] the offeror should be able to protect himself on costs and the offeree should not be troubled with the difficult choices that had to be made under the old rules.

An offer to settle the whole of a mixed claim

7.3 The foregoing discussion has been directed to attempts made to settle *part* of a mixed claim. A defendant to a mixed claim may wish to make an offer which is designed to dispose of the *whole claim* and afford him protection on costs if it is not accepted.

7.4 If he wishes to make *solely a money offer* in respect of the *whole claim*, he can do so by making a Part 36 payment in the normal way. If he wishes, say, to offer an undertaking or to consent to an injunction as his response to the *whole claim*, he can make a Part 36 offer to that effect.[8] If, however, he wants to make a substantive offer in respect of *each part* of the *whole claim* in a way that *disposes of the whole claim*, the new rules make specific provision for this situation.

7.5 Essentially, what is required is the making of a Part 36 payment in relation to the money claim and the Part 36 offer in relation to the non-money claim,[9] the two elements being linked by the terms of the Part 36 payment notice. That notice must—

(a) identify the document setting out the terms of the Part 36 offer; and

(b) state that acceptance of the Part 36 payment will be treated as acceptance also of the Part 36 offer.[10]

---

[5] See Chap. 6.
[6] See Chap. 4.
[7] For the possibility of seeking clarification of either, see Chap. 8.
[8] para. 7.2, above.
[9] r.36.4(2).
[10] r.36.4(3).

Notice of acceptance of the Part 36 payment in respect of which such a   7.6
Part 36 payment notice has been served will result in the Part 36 offer also
being accepted.[11] The practical consequences of acceptance will be dealt
with later[12] as will the costs consequences where one part of the offer is
"beaten by" the claimant and the other is not.[13]

---

[11] r.36.4(4).
[12] See Chap. 9.
[13] See Chap. 11.

CHAPTER 8

Clarification of Part 36 offers and payment notices

Introduction

8.1 The rules have been drafted so that the essential information about an offer that an offeree requires in order to give it proper consideration will be given in the Part 36 offer or the Part 36 payment notice.[1] The more clearly the terms are spelled out, the less likelihood there will be for post-settlement argument.[2] However, there may be circumstances where some clarification of the offer or payment notice is required. The rules provide for that situation.

The rule

8.2 Rule 36.9(1) entitles an offeree, within seven days of a Part 36 offer or payment being made, to "request the offeror to clarify the offer or payment notice". If the clarification is not given within seven days of a request, the court can be asked to make an order to that effect provided that the trial has not started.[3] The application for a "clarification order" must be made in accordance with Part 23 and the application notice "should state the respects in which the terms of a Part 36 offer or Part 36 notice, as the case may be, are said to need clarification".[4] If the court makes the order it must specify the date when the Part 36 offer or payment "is to be treated as having been made".[5] This will presumably normally be from the date when the clarification is received by the offeree.

---

[1] See Chap. 4.
[2] Often the outward manifestation of "post-settlement remorse", a syndrome identified by the Court of Appeal in *Arthur S. Hall & Co. v. Simons and Ors, The Times*, December 18, 1998, a case dealing with the important issue of "forensic immunity".
[3] r.36.9(2).
[4] Part 36 Practice Direction, paras 7.2 and 7.3
[5] r.36.9(3).

The rule is framed to permit clarification of "the offer or payment notice" 8.3
and the Practice Direction refers to clarification of the "terms" of the offer
or payment notice. It is unlikely that the court will wish to encourage
detailed and wide-ranging questions about an offer made under the guise of
seeking "clarification". Whilst it is impossible to be definitive at this stage,
it is likely that the court will, in the first instance, ask itself the broad
question of whether making the order will help the parties to settle the
whole or part of the case.[6] This may narrow down to the issue of whether
the terms of the offer or notice are in any material respect unclear or
ambiguous such that the offeree would be at a disadvantage in considering
it. If that is indeed the conclusion that the court forms, a clarification order
would be likely. The jurisdiction is, however, probably more flexible than
the provision under the old rules which permitted merely the making of an
order directing a defendant to amend his notice of payment to show how
much of a single sum paid in respect of two or more causes of action was
attributable to each cause of action. The court could do this only if the
plaintiff was "embarrassed" by the unapportioned payment.[7]

The offeree's options and their impact on costs

The question will arise of what an offeree should do when the offeror 8.4
neglects to specify in his offer or notice something that the rules require
him to specify. Examples would be a failure to state that a counterclaim or
an interim payment had been taken into account. Given that the rules do
state expressly that these matters be specified,[8] the chances are that the
omission was an oversight which a request for clarification would reveal
immediately. From a purely contractual point of view, the offeror will be
entitled to accept the offer as it stands and, subject to any issues as to
mistake or misrepresentation, the contract thus formed will be binding.
However, if he elects not to accept the offer, it is unlikely that the court
would be receptive to the argument, when the issue of costs is determined
at the end of the trial, that the offer was not accepted because it was
unclear or ambiguous. The remedy for that problem is the seeking of
clarification and the failure to do so, where it was plainly appropriate,
would undoubtedly be one of the "circumstances"[9] that could be taken
into account on costs. The culture embodied in the new rules demands a
sensible and meaningful dialogue.

---

[6] r.1.4(2)(f).
[7] Ord. 22, r.1(5). See Foskett, *op cit.*, paras 10–03—10–05.
[8] See Chap. 4.
[9] r.44.3(4).

CHAPTER 9

Acceptance other than with the court's permission

Introduction

9.1 The rules provide for certain automatic consequences to follow when a Part 36 offer or a Part 36 payment is accepted within the time allowed for acceptance.[1] The circumstances in which an offer may be accepted with the permission of the court after the period has expired will be addressed later.[2]

The mechanics of acceptance

9.2 A Part 36 offer (whether by a defendant or a claimant) or a Part 36 payment must be accepted by a "written notice of acceptance".[3] The rules require that this notice is "given" to the offeror,[4] which simply means that it must be sent (by whatever means of communication is appropriate) to the offeror. Any such notice must also be filed[5] with the court.[6] The contract formed by the acceptance of the offer will be concluded when notice of acceptance is received by the offeror.[7] The need for filing the notice with the court is for case management purposes only.

---

[1] The time will usually be 21 days from the date of the receipt of the offer or Part 36 payment notice (see para. 6.7 *et seq.*, above), though it would be open to an offeror to specify a longer period in relation to a Part 36 offer and the parties could agree to extend the time for acceptance of a Part 36 payment under r.2.11. The court may also order an extension or shortening of time for compliance with any rule: r.3.1(2)(a). It would be unlikely that the court would extend or shorten the time for acceptance of the Part 36 offer without the agreement of the offeror: to do so would offend the principle of freedom of contract.

[2] Chap. 10.

[3] rr.36.11(1) and 36.12(1).

[4] *ibid.*

[5] *i.e.* delivering it, by post or otherwise, to the Court Office: r.2.3(1).

[6] Part 36 Practice Direction, para.8.6.

[7] r.36.8(5).

The form of the notice of acceptance in respect of a Part 36 payment is **9.3**
provided for in a form which contains also a request for payment.[8] The
Practice Direction indicates[9] that the notice of acceptance in respect of a
Part 36 offer must also contain the same details as appear on that form: the
claim number, the title of the proceedings, the identity of the Part 36 offer
to which it relates and the signature of the offeree or his legal
representative.

The costs consequences of acceptance of a defendant's offer

Where a claimant accepts a Part 36 offer or a Part 36 payment relating to **9.4**
the *whole claim* within the prescribed time for acceptance, he "will be
entitled to his costs of the proceedings up to the date of serving notice of
acceptance".[10] Those costs include any costs attributable to the defendant's
counterclaim provided that the Part 36 offer or Part 36 payment notice
states that it takes account of the counterclaim.[11] The costs will be assessed
on the standard basis if not agreed.[12]

Where the Part 36 offer or Part 36 payment relates to *part only* of the **9.5**
claim and the claimant, at the time of serving notice of acceptance,
abandons the balance of the claim, then the claimant will again be entitled
to his costs on the basis referred to in the preceding paragraph "unless the
court orders otherwise".[13] The purpose of the inclusion of the proviso is to
permit a defendant to apply to the court for a different order from the
normal order if he considers it appropriate to do so having regard to the
costs associated with the abandoned parts of the claim. Under the old
rules,[14] the plaintiff who accepted the sum paid into court in respect of one
cause of action and abandoned the others was entitled to "his costs of the
action incurred up to the time of giving notice of acceptance." The "costs
of the action" embraced all the costs associated with the proceedings
including those referable to the abandoned causes of action. Since the court
had no discretion in the matter, this could cause an injustice.[15] The proviso
enables the court to make a more just order if invited to do so.

Where the Part 36 offer or Part 36 payment relates to *part only* of the **9.6**
claim, but the claimant does not abandon the other parts, the court will
decide who is liable for the costs unless the parties have agreed.[16]

---

[8] See Appendix III.
[9] para. 8.7.
[10] r.36.13(1).
[11] r.36.13(3).
[12] r.36.13(4). A costs order will be deemed to have been made on the standard basis:
r.44.12(1)(b).
[13] r.36.13(2).
[14] RSC, Ord. 62, r.5(4).
[15] *Hudson v. Elmbridge Borough Council* [1991] 1 W.L.R. 880, CA.
[16] r.36.15(3).

The costs consequences of acceptance of an offer or payment by one or more of several defendants[17]

9.7 Where a Part 36 offer or a Part 36 payment relates to a claim brought against a number of defendants *jointly or in the alternative*[18] and is made by one or more, but not all, of those defendants, the claimant will be entitled to his costs on the basis previously described[19] provided that:

    (a) he discontinues the claim against the other defendants; and

    (b) those other defendants consent in writing to the acceptance of the offer for payment.[20]

9.8 In this situation all the defendants are content with the acceptance by the claimant of the sum offered and that he should have his costs. Equally, the claimant is content not to continue his claims against those who were not directly party to the offer or payment. As between the defendants there may, of course, be outstanding disputes — for example, as to contribution or indemnity. Where the claimant is not prepared to discontinue his claim against the other defendants, or where one or more of them is or are not prepared to agree to the acceptance of the offer or payment, the claimant will require an order of the court permitting him to take the money out of court. At that time the Court will make such order as to costs as it considers appropriate.[21]

9.9 Where a claimant has pursued a number of defendants jointly or alternatively (or indeed jointly *and* alternatively), it would be unusual for there to remain anything in issue between him and those defendants once a settlement has been achieved with one or more of the defendants.[22] Where, however, *several liability*[23] is alleged against some or all of those defendants, the position is different. Several liability connotes a separate claim and where a claimant accepts a Part 36 offer or payment in respect of such a claim, but in the specified time for acceptance, he may do so without the court's permission and he will be entitled to his costs as well as being able

---

[17] For an analysis of the old rules, upon which the new rules are largely modelled, see Foskett, *op cit.*, para.10–26 *et seq.* See also *Carrs Bury St Edmunds Ltd v. Whitworth Partnership, etc.* (1997) 13 Const.L.J. 199, where *Hodgson v. Guardall* [1991] 3 All E.R. 823, was not followed.

[18] "Joint liability" is described in the Glossary as being a situation in which "parties . . . share a single liability" for which each can be held wholly liable. The expression "sued jointly" was interpreted under the former rules as being sued "in respect of a joint liability", not merely being joined together in the same proceedings: *Townsend v. Stone Toms & Partners* [1981] 1 W.L.R. 1153, CA.

[19] para. 9.4, above.

[20] r.36.17(2).

[21] r.36.17(4).

[22] See, *e.g.*, *Morris v. Wentworth-Stanley, The Times*, October 2, 1998; (1998) C.A.T. 1335. But see para. 10.5, below.

[23] "A person who is severally liable with others may remain liable for the whole claim even where judgment has been obtained against the others": Glossary.

to continue with a separate claim against the others provided that the law permits this in the particular context.[24] The costs to which the claimant will be entitled are, as already indicated,[25] the "costs of the proceedings up to the date of serving notice of acceptance". This is likely to be interpreted as the costs attributable to the claim against the particular defendant whose several liability is discharged by acceptance of his offer or payment. In other words, the expression "costs of the proceedings" would be limited to the costs of proceedings against *that* defendant in respect of *that* liability.[26]

The costs consequences of acceptance of a claimant's offer

Where a claimant's Part 36 offer is accepted within the period set for acceptance, the claimant will be entitled to his costs of the proceedings to the date upon which the defendant serves notice of acceptance.[27] His right to costs in this situation results in a deemed order that he is entitled to those costs on the standard basis.[28]

9.10

The mechanics of payment out

In those cases where a Part 36 payment is accepted and the costs consequences are automatic, the claimant obtains payment out to him of the sum in court by making a request for payment by means of the relevant form.[29] The form should be filed with the court and there may be other formalities to consider depending on whether the request for payment is made to the Royal Courts of Justice or elsewhere and whether the claimant wants a cheque or a direct transfer to his bank account.[30] The payment will be made to the claimant's legal representative if he is represented or direct to him unless he has been in receipt of Legal Aid at any time in respect of

9.11

---

[24] r.36.17(3). The published version of this rule was modified subsequently in the light of the decision of the House of Lords in *Jameson v. Central Electricity Generating Board* [1999] 2 W.L.R. 141 which holds that a settlement with one of a number of several tortfeasors discharges the whole claim.

[25] para. 9.4, above.

[26] The previous rule, which governed the situation hitherto, used the expression "costs of the action" (Ord. 62, r.5(4)). That was interpreted as referring to the costs of the action "against that defendant": *Q.B.E. Ltd v. Mediterranean Insurance, etc.* [1992] 1 W.L.R. 573; *Carrs Bury St Edmunds Ltd v. Whitworth Partnership, etc.*, above. This was to prevent possible injustice to a paying in defendant. It is submitted that the expression "costs of the proceedings" is even more susceptible to this interpretation than was the expression "costs of the action". A defendant who wishes to make the position absolutely clear might wish to phrase his Part 36 payment notice in a way which demonstrates that the payment is made in respect of that "part of the claim" which relates to him.

[27] r.36.14.

[28] r.44.12(1)(c).

[29] r.36.16. The form appears in Appendix III.

[30] Practice Direction, paras 9.1–9.4

the proceedings, when the payment will be made to the Legal Aid Board by direction of the court.[31]

Interest

9.12 If the first Part 36 payment made by a defendant is accepted, no interest will have accrued whilst it is in court because it will not have been transmitted to an investment account.[32] If, however, an increased Part 36 payment is accepted within the period for acceptance, interest will have accrued on any sum or sums previously paid into court. Unless the parties have agreed otherwise, accrued interest to the date of acceptance will be paid to the defendant and any interest accruing from the date of acceptance until payment out will be paid to the claimant.[33]

Consequences of acceptance for the proceedings

9.13 Where a Part 36 *payment* which relates to the *whole claim* is accepted, the claim will be stayed.[34] Where the payment expressly took into account any counterclaim,[35] the effect of acceptance will be to stay all proceedings including the counterclaim. There is no reason to suppose that the effect and operation of a stay thus imposed will be any different from that which obtained under the former rules.[36] The rules state expressly that any stay imposed in the situation described above will not affect the powers of the court to deal with any question of costs (including interest on costs[37]), or to order a payment out of court of any sum paid in.

9.14 Where a Part 36 *payment* relating to *part only* of the claim is accepted, the claim will be stayed as to that part. If the parties have not agreed the liability for the costs of that part of the claim, the court will decide the issue.[38] The same result will follow if a Part 36 *offer* relating to *part only* of a claim is accepted.[39] Although the rules do not state precisely what is to happen if a Part 36 *offer* relating to an *issue*[40] is accepted, it is likely that the purposive construction to be given to the rules[41] will result in the

---

[31] *ibid.*, para. 9.5.
[32] *ibid.*, paras 12.3 and 12.4.
[33] *ibid.*, para. 8.10.
[34] r.36.15(1). "A stay imposes a halt on proceedings, apart from taking steps allowed by the Rules or the terms of the stay. Proceedings can be continued if the stay is lifted": Glossary.
[35] Chap. 4, para. 4.11, above.
[36] Foskett, *op cit.*, para. 10–02.
[37] See *Electricity Supply Nominees Ltd v. Farrell and Ors*, [1997] 1 W.L.R. 1149, CA.
[38] r.36.15(3). The court will doubtless have regard to its power to limit the costs to, for example, a proportion of the costs or to a "distinct part of the proceedings": r.44.3(6).
[39] *ibid.*
[40] para. 4.7, above.
[41] r.1.2(b).

expression "issue" being treated as coterminous with "part" for this purpose. Liability is usually seen as an "issue" in a claim. An agreement as to apportionment of liability resulting from the acceptance of a Part 36 offer will probably result, initially at least, in a stay of the proceedings in relation to that issue.[42]

When a Part 36 *offer* relating to the *whole* of the claim is accepted, the stay imposed by the rules will be "upon the terms of the offer" and either party can apply to the court "to enforce those terms without the need for a new claim."[43] The effect is to translate the agreement into a rule-imposed Tomlin order,[44] although the stay is imposed *by the rules* and not by an order of the court as such. The equivalent of the former "liberty to apply" is, for this purpose, a right given by the rules to apply to the court for the purposes of enforcement. There may be circumstances in which the parties do require there to be some kind of order to give effect to their agreement: they might want a Tomlin *order* as such or, perhaps, an order incorporating an undertaking to the court or a declaration. The latter may be required particularly in the context of the acceptance by a claimant of an offer in relation to *both aspects* of a mixed claim under rule 36.4.[45] An *order* in relation to costs or Legal Aid taxation may also be required. If this is what is specified in the Part 36 offer which is then accepted, the stay imposed by the rules will simply be upon the "term" that the parties co-operate in seeking an order by consent in the agreed terms. That term will be "implied" into the agreement if it is not expressed.[46] **9.15**

Where a Part 36 offer has been accepted an agreement will have been concluded. Enforcement of that agreement will normally take place by means of an application (made in accordance with Part 23) for a suitable order pursuant to such rule as permits the order to be made.[47] A claim for damages arising from a breach of the agreement might be interpreted as something other than an application for "enforcement" of the agreement. Indeed this was the view of the Court of Appeal in *Hollingsworth v.* **9.16**

---

[42] The agreement will probably be translated into a judgment on the issue as to liability (either 100 per cent or in some lesser proportion) at a later stage.

[43] r.36.15(2).

[44] See further at para. 9.16, below. Also Foskett, *op cit.*, paras 5–11 *et seq.* The author claims (immodestly) some credit for the inclusion in Part 36 of this provision which seemed to be the sensible practical response to the particular situation. He regrets, though, failure to keep the name "Tomlin" alive in the body of the rules at r.40.6(3)(b)(ii). In several early drafts of Part 40 the words "a Tomlin order" appeared in parenthesis at the end of this sub-paragraph and remained there without objection from the Civil Procedure Rule Committee. It was, however, eventually spotted and upon the last occasion Part 40 was considered by the Committee these words were excised on the basis that if "Anton Piller" and "Mareva" had to go, so did "Tomlin"!

[45] para. 7.5, above.

[46] Foskett, *op cit.*, paras 5.15 *et seq.* The parties may be able to utilise r.40.6 in appropriate circumstances: see Chap. 14.

[47] r.36.15(2).

Humphrey[48] in relation to a claim for damages arising from the breach of the agreement contained in the schedule to a Tomlin order. The result of that view was that a fresh action was needed in order to pursue that claim for damages. In order to prevent the somewhat cumbersome process of starting wholly new proceedings in the event of a breach of a term of an accepted Part 36 offer, provision is made in the rules that such a remedy may be claimed "by applying to the court without the need to start a new claim unless the court orders otherwise".[49]

---

[48] (1987) C.A.T. 1244; *The Independent*, December 21, 1987. See Foskett, *op cit.*, para. 15–16 and 15–17. Where parties agree a Tomlin order (rather than having the effect of one imposed on them pursuant to the rules), they may wish to overcome the consequences of *Hollingsworth v. Humphrey* by agreeing that a new claim is not required if a claim for breach of the agreement has to be pursued: see Appendix VII.

[49] r.36.15(6). The proviso "unless the court orders otherwise" entitles the court to direct a new claim, or some other form of proceeding than merely an application, if it considers it necessary and appropriate to do so.

42

CHAPTER 10

Acceptance with the court's permission

Introduction

In Chapter 9 consideration was given to the costs and other consequences **10.1** arising from acceptance of a Part 36 offer or payment when the permission of the court prior to acceptance was *not* required. Consideration will now be given to the circumstances in which the permission of the court *is* required to enable acceptance and the consequences that do, or may, flow from the grant (or refusal) of that permission.

Children and patients

Consistent with previous practice,[1] any settlement or compromise of a **10.2** claim brought by or against a child or patient requires the approval of the court for it to be valid.[2] This means, in effect, that any Part 36 offer or Part 36 payment (and indeed any pre-action offer) could not be accepted without the permission of the court.[3] The rules prescribe the practice to be adopted in order to obtain the court's approval[4] and they give the court power to direct how any money recovered by or on behalf or for the benefit of a child or patient is to be invested or otherwise dealt with.[5] Where permission to accept a Part 36 payment is given, whether before or after the trial has started, no money can be paid out of court without an order of the court.[6] Where permission is given before the trial begins, the court will doubtless make an appropriate order as to costs. Where

---

[1] RSC, Ord. 18; CCR, Ord. 10.
[2] r.21.10(1).
[3] r.36.18(1).
[4] r.21.10(2).
[5] r.21.11.
[6] rr.36.18(1)(b) and 36.18(2)(a).

43

permission is given after the trial has begun, the court must "deal with the whole costs of the proceedings" in any order it makes.[7]

10.3 The effect upon the proceedings of permission being given to accept a Part 36 offer or Part 36 payment in relation to a child or patient will be the same as in any other case,[8] except that any stay that would otherwise arise on its acceptance will take effect only when the approval of the court has been given.[9]

10.4 So far as the costs consequences of acceptance are concerned, it is unlikely that they will differ to any material extent from the consequences that apply in litigation not involving a child or patient, certainly if the decision to accept the offer or payment into court subject to the approval of the court is intimated or made to the offeror within the normal time for acceptance. The position with regard to costs if permission is sought beyond that time is dealt with later,[10] as is the position if a child or patient claimant fails to improve on the Part 36 offer or payment.[11]

Several defendants

10.5 The circumstances in which a claimant may accept a Part 36 offer or part 36 payment made by one or more, but not all, of several defendants without needing the permission of the court have been described.[12] In any case other than those described the claimant must apply to the court for an order permitting payment out to him of the sum in court.[13] The purpose of this requirement, which largely mirrors the requirements of the old rules,[14] is to enable the court to resolve any outstanding issue as to costs. An example of a situation in which the court might be required to adjudicate is where the claimant wants to accept a Part 36 payment made by one of two defendants sued *in the alternative*, but there is an issue between the paying in defendant and the claimant as to who should be responsible for the costs of the other defendant. Under the former practice, the question as to primary liability for those costs was resolved on the basis of whether it was reasonable for the plaintiff to have joined the defendant whose costs are in issue. Once that had been resolved in the plaintiff's favour the remaining matter for consideration was whether the non-paying in defendant

---

[7] r.36.18(2)(b).
[8] para. 9.13 *et seq.*, above.
[9] r.36.15(4).
[10] See para. 10.6 *et seq.*, below.
[11] para. 11.8, below.
[12] paras 9.7–9.9, above.
[13] r.36.17(4).
[14] RSC, Ord. 22, r.4.

recovered his costs directly against the paying in defendant or against the plaintiff who then recovered them against the paying in defendant.[15] Issues of that kind will continue to arise in the future, although under a case-managed system it is likely that the presence of a particular party within the proceedings will have been addressed at an early stage. That may result in a less mechanistic, more flexible and better informed approach to this kind of dispute as to costs. The making of an order as to costs on the giving of permission for acceptance of a Part 36 payment will doubtless reflect that approach.

Late Part 36 offer or payment and/or late acceptance

As already indicated,[16] the only circumstance in which a Part 36 offer or Part 36 payment can be accepted without obtaining the court's permission is when it is *made* at least 21 days before the trial and is then *accepted* within the time prescribed (usually 21 days from the date it was made). In every other case, the court's permission is required for acceptance *unless the parties agree the liability as to costs.*   **10.6**

So that an appreciation of the difference between the former practice and the new practice can be obtained, it is worth restating the approach to a late payment into court made by a defendant, or the late acceptance by a plaintiff of a timeously-made payment into court, under the former rules. A late payment into court could be accepted by a plaintiff with the usual consequences as to costs at any time prior to the commencement of the trial.[17] A payment into court made in good time could be accepted by a plaintiff after the usual 21-day period, albeit only with the leave of the court, that leave almost invariably being granted provided that his prospects of success had not materially worsened since the date of the payment into court and also upon the terms that the plaintiff paid the defendant's costs after the time for acceptance had expired.[18] Furthermore, the former rules permitted the making by a defendant of a payment into court (or an increased payment into court) after the trial had begun which the plaintiff could accept within two days and obtain his costs in consequence.[19]   **10.7**

In each of the foregoing situations the costs consequences of the acceptance of the payment into court were clear to both sides. That made evaluation of the offer constituted by the payment into court tolerably easy and the overall settlement the more easily achieved. The removal of the   **10.8**

---

[15] See, *e.g., Goldsworthy v. Brickell* [1987] Ch. 378 at 418.

[16] paras 6.7–6.9, above.

[17] Chap. 6, n.23. If the late payment into court was caused by the failure of the plaintiff to give proper particulars of and information to support his case, there might have been arguments on the taxation of costs about what was or was not recoverable. However, the principle was clear: the plaintiff could obtain his costs to be taxed if not agreed.

[18] See para. 3.13, above.

[19] Chap. 6, n.23.

certainty offered by the former rules is potentially controversial. Some may ask how the creation of a degree of uncertainty, by requiring the court's permission for acceptance (a permission which, theoretically, could be withheld) and leaving open the court's discretion as to costs, can assist in achieving the desired objective of encouraging the settlement of cases.

10.9 It should, of course, be recalled that the prime objective is the *early* settlement of cases.[20] The observance of pre-action protocols and the court's active intervention in the management of a case once proceedings have started are designed to ensure that the wherewithal to achieve early settlement of a case is available. If a defendant, for example, is not able to make an informed and worthwhile offer well before the trial, the court's case management functions will arguably have failed in their intended purpose. If a claimant is unable to evaluate an offer made well before the trial, the same comment might be made. To that extent it is, therefore, logical that the rules which provide the framework for a case-managed system of civil justice should not contain provisions the existence of which might constitute an encouragement to parties not to co-operate with that system.[21] In a nutshell, therefore, that is the rationale for the omission from the new rules of provisions similar to those in the old.

10.10 Notwithstanding the need for the rules to reflect the philosophy of early settlement, there will remain those cases which, even in the best case-managed system, will not be capable of settlement until shortly before or during the trial. Indeed this is, perhaps, easier to envisage when a lengthy trial is in progress than it is shortly before the commencement of one destined to be of fairly short duration. Case management techniques are unlikely to reveal how well a witness is likely to perform before he or she takes to the witness box. A defendant who feels that the credibility of a main witness for the claimant is likely to be damaged significantly in cross-examination, but whose expectations in this regard are unfulfilled, may feel that the time has arrived when a significant advance on a previous offer is necessary. Equally, a claimant the credibility of whose case *has* been undermined substantially may look with longing at an unwithdrawn Part 36 offer or Part 36 payment. The court will undoubtedly from time to time be confronted with applications for permission to accept an offer or payment in this kind of situation. Equally, there will be cases where, for some reason, a defendant has not been willing or able to make an offer or payment into court until shortly before the trial which, as it happens, the claimant would like to accept. Where the liability for costs is agreed, then no problem exists in any of these situations.[22] How, though, will a court respond where there is no agreement as to costs?

---

[20] Chap. 1.
[21] See para. 4.33, Minutes of the Civil Procedure Rule Committee meeting of September 17, 1998.
[22] para. 10.6, above.

46

It is, of course, impossible to give an answer that will cover every situation. **10.11**
In exercising any power given to it by the rules, the court must seek to give
effect to the overriding objective.[23] Save to the extent that the court will
want to ensure that the issue left between the parties is dealt with justly,
there is no real guidance to be obtained by reference to the overriding
objective. It is, perhaps, possible to envisage a situation in which both
parties have been at fault in causing the delay in addressing settlement and,
accordingly, "the need to allot [the court's] resources to other cases" may
have a bearing on the permission sought. However, the starting point in
every case will be to proceed on the assumption that both parties are
content with the sum of money or the terms offered, one of the terms in
either case being that the court will decide on the order as to costs.[24] It is
very difficult to envisage any situation in which the court would decline to
grant a claimant permission to accept a Part 36 offer or Part 36 payment
unless (i) the time for acceptance had expired and (ii) his prospects of
success in the proceedings have materially worsened.[25] So far as the
question of costs is concerned, it is likely that the starting point would be
the proposition that the claimant has had to bring the proceedings in order
to obtain the offer made and that, accordingly, he is to be treated as the
successful party and thus entitled to his costs.[26] If, however, the claimant
was himself largely responsible for impeding the defendant's ability to
make a reasonable offer until very late in the day, that would doubtless be
a factor for the court to reflect in the costs order. The court's full
discretion as to costs would exist in this situation and it would, presumably, be open to the offeror to raise any point as to the costs of the
proceedings that he wishes when the offeree seeks permission from the
court to accept the offer.

Because of the open-ended nature of the court's discretion on costs, it is **10.12**
likely that the parties will endeavour to agree who should bear the costs
and to what extent. However, when the defendant is not minded to agree
that the claimant should have all his costs (which would, of course, be
subject to assessment in the absence of agreement as to the amount), it may
be good practice for the defendant to spell out at the time he makes his late
Part 36 offer or Part 36 payment how he would invite the court to exercise
its discretion in the absence of agreement.[27] The court's discretion will not
necessarily be exercised in that way, but this approach will enable the
claimant to know (i) what would be acceptable to the defendant and (ii)
the probable outer limit of any adverse costs consequences from his point
of view.

---

[23] r.1.2.
[24] This kind of arrangement is not unknown under the former practice: see Foskett, *op cit.*,
para. 15–03. However, its disadvantage was perceived to be the uncertainty of the outcome
from the parties' point of view and the difficulty of knowing how to reach the correct
conclusion from the court's point of view.
[25] The same approach would probably apply in respect of a *claimant's* Part 36 offer also:
r.36.12(2) and (3).
[26] r.44.3(2).
[27] Precedent No. 12.

10.13 In those cases where the court is left to decide the question of costs, it will doubtless need to strike a balance between doing what is right in the particular case and not setting some kind of precedent that makes settlement in other cases more difficult. It is an area where a practice will doubtless develop as the case-managed system itself develops.

CHAPTER 11

Failing to beat a Part 36 offer or Part 36 payment

Introduction

A trial which achieves nothing more than had previously been offered can **11.1** be an expensive affair. An appreciation of this fact constitutes an incentive to settle except for the few with unlimited resources.[1] Although the former rules merely required the existence of a payment into court to be taken into account in the exercise of the court's discretion as to costs, it became the established practice that a payment into court was the dominant consideration in a damages claim.[2] The general rule was that a plaintiff who beat the payment into court obtained his costs,[3] but a plaintiff who did not obtained his costs only to the date of the payment into court and had to pay the defendant's costs thereafter. This general principle has found expression in the new rules in relation to offers made by a defendant.

Defendant's offer — money claim

A defendant to a money claim must make a Part 36 payment to secure the **11.2** protection afforded by Part 36.[4] If the claimant fails to "better"[5] a Part 36 payment, then the normal result will be that he will be ordered to pay the defendant's costs "after the latest date on which the payment . . . could have been accepted without needing the permission of the court."[6] As the

---

[1] *Cutts v. Head* [1984] Ch. 290; *Roache v. News Group Newspapers Ltd, The Times,* November 23, 1992.
[2] Foskett, *op cit.*, para. 10–19.
[3] But see *Charm Maritime Inc. v. Elborne Mitchell*, referred to at para. 12.2, below.
[4] para. 6.1, above.
[5] r.36.20(1)(a). "Matching" it will not suffice. But see Chap. 12.
[6] r.36.20(2).

successful party[7] to that date, he will be entitled to his costs. Since the effect of the rules is to permit a claimant 21 days in which to give notice of acceptance,[8] it is more equitable that any costs reasonably incurred by him during that time (which will, of course, be subject to assessment) should be paid by the defendant. This may have an important bearing on the amount of costs actually payable if a Part 36 payment is left until a date only just outside the 21-day period before trial.

11.3 The normal order referred to above will be made unless the court "considers it unjust to do so".[9] The considerations to be taken into account in determining whether it would be "unjust" so to order are referred to below.[10]

Defendant's offer — non-money claim

11.4 The equivalent of the need to "better" a Part 36 payment in the context of a Part 36 offer is "to obtain a judgment which is more advantageous" than the offer.[11] During consideration of the new rules the word "materially" appeared before the word "advantageous" for a while. However, it was eventually rejected on the basis that it could lead to unnecessary argument.[12] The question, therefore, that a court needs to ask is simply whether the claimant has secured something "more advantageous" than was previously offered. Given the possible approach of the court to the bettering of a Part 36 payment by only a minimal amount,[13] it is possible to envisage the need to ask the question in some cases whether the marginal advantage conferred by the decision of the court over that which was previously offered is such as to warrant an order for costs in a claimant's favour[14].

11.5 If the claimant fulfils the requirement of obtaining a judgment which is "more advantageous" than the offer, he will be awarded his costs. If he fails, the normal result in the case of an unbettered Part 36 payment will arise[15] subject to the court ordering the contrary because it "considers it unjust" that the usual order is made.[16]

---

[7] r.44.3(2).
[8] para. 6.7, above.
[9] r.36.20(2).
[10] para. 11.8 et seq., below.
[11] r.36.20(1)(b).
[12] para. 4.50, Minutes of Civil Procedure Rule Committee meeting of September 17, 1998.
[13] paras 12.2–12.3, below.
[14] The test is not substantially different from that applied to *Calderbank* offers prior to the implementation of the new rules. The question posed by Sir Thomas Bingham M.R., as he then was, in *Roache v. News Group Newspapers Ltd*, above, was as follows: "Who, as a matter of substance and reality, had won? Has the plaintiff won anything of value which he could not have won without fighting the action through to the finish?" This approach was subsequently adopted in *Butcher v. Wolfe* and *Hobin v. Douglas, The Times,* December 9 and 29, 1998, respectively. *cf. Everglade Maritime Inc. v. The Schiffahrtsgesellschaft, etc., "The Maria"* [1993] Q.B. 780.
[15] para. 11.2, above.
[16] para. 11.3, above.

Defendant's offer — mixed claim[17]

Where a defendant offers, say, an undertaking in response to a mixed claim **11.6**
(and makes no Part 36 payment in relation to the money claim), or makes a
Part 36 payment in response to the money claim but offers no undertaking
in response to the non-money claim,[18] the offer will fall to be judged
initially by reference to whether the court awards some substantive relief
on that part of the claim in relation to which no offer or Part 36 payment
was made. If the court does so, the claimant will have bettered the offer or
obtained a "more advantageous" judgment than the defendant's offer. If,
however, no substantive relief is awarded on that element of the claim
then, subject to the Part 36 offer or Part 36 payment (whichever is
relevant) being more advantageous or better than the court's award, the
claimant will have failed in beating the defendant's offer of settlement. The
normal order will presumably be made in that situation subject to the
"unjust" proviso[19].

Where the defendant makes an offer pursuant to rule 36.4,[20] each aspect of **11.7**
the offer will have to be judged by reference to the test applicable to the
relevant part of the offer. Is the Part 36 offer in respect of the non-money
"more advantageous" than the court's award? Is the Part 36 payment
"better" than the court's award? If the claimant fails to beat *both* features
of the offer of settlement, the normal order (subject to the "unjust"
proviso) will be made. Where the claimant beats one, but not the other,
then the court will doubtless have to take a much broader view of its
discretion in relation to costs than the more mechanistic view that would
derive from a failure to beat both parts of the overall offer.

Departure from general rule on grounds of injustice

As indicated above,[21] the normal order made upon the failure of a claimant **11.8**
to achieve more than a previous Part 36 offer or Part 36 payment can be
displaced if the court "considers it unjust" for that order to be made. Part
36 gives no direct guidance as such on what might make it unjust for the
normal order to be made.[22] Since there is an argument for saying that a
marginal improvement on a Part 36 offer or Part 36 payment should not

---

[17] See generally Chap. 7.
[18] para. 7.2, above.
[19] para. 11.8, below.
[20] para. 7.5, above.
[21] paras 11.3 and 11.5, above.
[22] *cf.* the position in relation to an award of enhanced interest and indemnity costs against a
defendant when a claimant does better than his offer: para. 11.14 *et seq*, below. The factors
specified in r.36.21(5) may well be applicable more generally than simply in relation to
claimants' offers.

necessarily entitle the claimant to all his costs,[23] there may be a countervailing argument that a very narrow "miss" should not result in the very significant penalty as to costs which the normal order might cause in a particular case.[24]

Failing to "beat" a claimant's offer

11.9 It is debatable whether the failure of a defendant to secure an award to a claimant of less than the claimant's offer represents a failure to "beat" that offer. However, this is a convenient point to note the consequences.

11.10 A claimant can make a pre-action offer[25] or one that is made after the proceedings have begun. In essence he will be offering to settle at a lesser figure, or upon less onerous terms to the defendant, than appears in his claim. If the defendant accepts the offer then the dispute is ended. If the defendant makes a counter-offer which the claimant accepts, the dispute also comes to an end. If, however, the claim proceeds unresolved, various possible outcomes may be envisaged. First, the claimant achieves less than his offer, but more than any offer or Part 36 payment made by the defendant. In this situation, the claimant is still prima facie to be regarded as the successful party and entitled to his costs, subject to the court exercising its discretion in some way adverse to him if, for example, he "exaggerated his claim".[26] Secondly, the claimant may achieve less than his offer and less than the defendant's offer or Part 36 payment. In this situation, it is likely that he will obtain his costs to the expiration of the period for acceptance of the defendant's offer or Part 36 payment and that he will be ordered to pay the defendant's costs thereafter.[27] Finally, of course, the claimant may achieve more than his offer. What consequences flow from this?

11.11 If the result was purely that the claimant obtained his costs in the normal way, there would be no incentive to him to make any concession by way of an offer and little incentive to the defendant to accept it. Prior to the new rules, the court was, in some circumstances, prepared to award a plaintiff indemnity costs after the date of expiry of the offer if the offer was ultimately bettered at trial.[28] The rationale was, presumably, that an

---

[23] Chap. 12.
[24] However, there are significant arguments against taking that kind of approach: see para. 12.4, below. It is unlikely that the fact that the claimant is a child or a patient and that his compensation would be reduced substantially by the normal order would be a reason for holding the normal order to be "unjust": *Abada v. Gray and anor, The Times*, July 9, 1997, CA.
[25] Chap. 3.
[26] r.44.3(5)(b).
[27] See paras 11.2–11.5, above.
[28] *McDonnell v. Woodhouse and Jones and Ors, The Times*, May 25, 1995, Waterhouse J.

unreasonable refusal of a reasonable offer designed to obviate the need for the continuation of the proceedings should not leave the plaintiff out of pocket. The opportunity to make such an order has been provided for expressly in the new rules[29] in the event of the defendant being held liable for more, or upon terms more advantageous to the claimant, than the proposals contained in the claimant's offer.[30]

Somewhat more controversially, the rules give the court in this situation to **11.12** award a higher than normal rate of interest on any sum of money awarded and upon any indemnity costs awarded.[31] Indeed the rules suggest that the court has an automatic obligation[32] to award a higher rate of interest on some part of the money award[33] and on the relevant part of the costs[34] unless it considers it unjust to do so. Subject to that latter proviso, there are two areas where the court has a discretion in operating this provision, the first relating to the amount of the sum of money to which, and the period over which, the higher rate of interest is applicable; the second being in relation to the actual rate of interest itself.

(i) The amount on which, and the period for which, increased interest is payable

The enhanced rate of interest may be ordered to be paid "on the whole or **11.13** part of any sum of money (excluding interest)[35] awarded to the claimant . . . or some or all of the period starting with the latest date on which the defendant could have accepted the offer without needing the permission of the court."[36] This gives the court a wide discretion in relation to the sum of money on which the increased interest can be paid. At the top end of the scale, the court could award increased interest on the *whole* amount of the award, not merely on the difference between the amount referred to in the

---

[29] r.36.21(3)(a).

[30] r.36.21(1).

[31] The controversy arises from a perception that a claimant who is awarded higher interest on his damages if he "beats" his own offer is the recipient of a windfall or uncovenanted bonus arising, in effect, from a previously placed wager. The loser is a defendant who is merely exercising his right to contest the claim. Whilst these concerns may continue to be entertained in some quarters, it should be borne in mind that the *maximum* level of additional interest potentially payable (10 per cent above base rate) is considerably less than was once proposed: *Access to Justice*, Final Report, para. 7.

[32] r.36.21(4) provides that where r.36.21(1) applies "the court *will* make the orders referred to in paragraphs (2) and (3) unless it considers it unjust to do so." (Emphasis added). This would seem to override the apparently discretionary nature of the power deriving from the use of the word "may" in r.36.21(2) and (3). Consistency of approach is achieved in this way.

[33] para. 11.13, below.

[34] Costs may be awarded on the indemnity basis in the circumstances provided for in this rule only "from the latest date when the defendant could have accepted the offer without needing the permission of the court": r.36.21(3)(a).

[35] Any interest included within the claimant's offer must be excluded from the operation of the rule otherwise interest on interest might be awarded. It should be noted that the power to award higher interest under this rule "is in addition to any other power it may have to award interest": r.36.21(6).

[36] r.36.21(2).

offer and the amount of the award. Equally, it can relate to any *part* of the sum awarded. The period over which it can be ordered is, however, confined to the period *after* the offer could have been accepted without needing the court's permission. The court can choose the whole or part of that period.

(ii) The rate of interest

11.14 The rule provides that the interest capable of being awarded may be "at a rate not exceeding 10 per cent above base rate".[37] This means that the court may add up to 10 per cent *to* the applicable base rate. It does not mean that the court is restricted to adding merely 10 per cent *of* the applicable base rate.[38] The rule does not specify the date on which the base rate is to be determined. If it has varied during the period between the date when the claimant's offer could have been accepted without the court's permission and the date of the award, doubtless an average could be taken.

(iii) How will these choices be made?

11.15 As with all powers conferred by the rules, the court must seek to give effect to the overriding objective when it makes its choice.[39] It is difficult at this stage to give any helpful guidance on how this power is likely to be exercised. Within the broad discretion conferred by the rules, a broad practice will doubtless emerge as the culture reflected in the new system comes to be established. The purpose of the rule, however, is to encourage both parties to focus on the resolution of the dispute, although doubtless any "penalty" effectively imposed on the defendant would have to be proportionate. It may be helpful to put forward an example of the practical effect that various choices might have upon a particular case. Some round-figure sums and clearly defined periods are taken for the sake of convenience.

The case

> C sues D for damages for personal injuries. Liability has been admitted. C's schedule discloses a total claim of about £300,000 comprising damages for pain, suffering and loss of amenities of life, a claim for loss of earnings to trial, certain other items of special damage and a claim for future loss of earnings. Because of the uncertainties over the loss of earnings claim, C offers to accept £225,000 (inclusive of interest to 21 days later[40]). D does not accept the offer and makes a Part 36 payment of £200,000. At a trial which concludes six months after the time for acceptance of C's offer expired, the court awards C a total of £250,000 before interest is

---

[37] r.36.21(2) and (3)(b).
[38] If the applicable base rate is, say, 6 per cent , the court could award interest up to the rate of 16 per cent. It would not be restricted to 6.6 per cent.
[39] r.1.2.
[40] r.36.22(1).

calculated. The constituent elements are £50,000 by way of damages for pain, suffering and loss of amenities of life, £55,000 for four years' loss of earnings from the accident to trial, £15,000 for various other items of special damage and £130,000 for future loss of earnings. The claim form was served two years before the trial and, accordingly, two years of interest at three per cent per annum is awarded in relation to the sum of £50,000. Interest is awarded at one-half of the full Special Investment Account rate (eight per cent) for the period of four years from the date of the accident to trial — *i.e.* 16 per cent cumulatively — making an award of interest of £11,200. The total award of the court, inclusive of interest, is £264,200.

Enhanced interest on the damages

The court concludes that it is not unjust to order increased interest on the damages. It can do so on the sum of £250,000 or any part of it for a period of six months. The base rate during the six month period was five per cent.

If it chooses the *maximum* it can award (15 per cent) on the total sum (£250,000) for the whole period of six months, the additional sum awarded would be £18,750. This would represent an approximate seven per cent uplift on the sum actually awarded by the court inclusive of interest. If it chooses five per cent above base rate (*i.e.* 10 per cent) for half that period, the additional sum awarded would be £6,250. This would represent an uplift of 2.36 per cent on the sum, inclusive of interest, awarded by the court. It should, of course, be realised that any interest that accrued on the sum of £200,000 in court for the six month period would revert to the defendant.[41] In other words, something like £8,000 would be repaid to the defendant and the defendant would have had the use of the balance of £50,000 during the same period.

Enhanced interest on indemnity costs

As a rule of thumb, indemnity costs have traditionally been thought to be about 20 per cent higher than the costs on a standard basis. If C's total costs from the expiry of his offer to the conclusion of the trial are £37,500, the effect of the order for indemnity costs itself will cost D a further £7,500 compared with what would have been paid on a standard basis. If the maximum rate of interest (15 per cent) was applied to the whole sum awarded by way of indemnity costs for the whole of the six month period and thereafter until payment following assessment (say, another six months), the amount of interest payable as a result would be £5,625. If costs had been assessed on the standard basis at £30,000, interest would normally have been payable from the conclusion of the trial, when the order for costs is made, at the judgment rate of eight per cent. If the assessment was concluded after six months, the interest payable would have been £1,200.

---

[41] See Part 36 Practice Direction, para. 7.10.

Unjust to make the Order?

11.16 The logical sequence of questions for the court to ask and answer would seem to be as follows:

(i) Has the claimant exceeded his offer?
(ii) If so, is it unjust for an order for enhanced interest to be made?
(iii) If not, what should the amount of that interest be, on what sum and for what period?

However it is likely that (ii) and (iii) will merge to some degree. Since the court is obliged to "take into account all the circumstances of the case", including certain specific matters, in deciding whether it would be unjust to make the orders for enhanced interest and indemnity costs,[42] one of the factors might arguably be the actual impact that the making of such an order would have.

11.17 The specific matters to which the court will have regard are the terms of the offer and the stage in the proceedings in which it was made, the information available to the parties at the time of the offer and the conduct of the parties with regard to the giving or refusing of information for the purpose of enabling the offer to be evaluated.[43] In the example given above, if C had failed to supply D with sufficient information to enable D to assess whether £225,000 was a reasonable settlement figure, it is highly unlikely that the court would penalise D. The rule is doubtless designed to benefit the claimant who makes a bona fide attempt to settle his claim at a reasonable figure. A failure to supply proper information can hardly be said to have been acting bona fide. Equally, the court is likely to be slow to assist a claimant who formulates an enormous claim, but who offers to accept something very small by comparison and then achieves slightly more than that figure. Again, this would hardly seem to be bona fide negotiation. A claimant who puts forward a whole series of offers (perhaps all on the same date), hoping that one will be exceeded so as to attract the benefits of the rule, is unlikely to receive an enthusiastic response from the court either.

---

[42] r.36.21(5).
[43] *ibid.*

CHAPTER 12

The narrow beating of, or failure to beat, a Part 36 offer or Part 36 payment

The normal consequences of bettering a Part 36 offer or payment have **12.1** been described previously.[1] The claimant will obtain his costs. Merely matching the offer will not, of course, result in it having been "bettered" and, accordingly, the claimant will face the same consequences as if he had failed to achieve the same as had previously been offered.

The question arises as to whether the bettering of a Part 36 offer or Part 36 **12.2** payment by a very narrow margin, particularly if the marginal success has been achieved at disproportionate expense, should entitle the claimant to all his costs. The issue is brought into relief by a case decided under the former rules.

> In *Charm Maritime Inc. v. Elborne Mitchell*[2] P sued D, its former solicitors, for damages of approximately $20 million representing its alleged losses arising from D's negligence in permitting P's claim in another action to be dismissed for want of prosecution. The trial lasted 30 days. One of the main issues was whether an allegation of fraud in the earlier action would have been sustained. Detailed expert accountancy reports were prepared, and lengthy expert evidence was given, in relation to this issue. The net result was that P achieved a judgment for $841,070. D had made payments into court totalling $822,368, the final increase being made in August 1995 before the trial commenced in the Autumn. P, therefore, "beat" the payment into court by about $19,000. The trial judge said that, on the assumption (which had to be made for the purposes of her decision) that P had beaten the payment into court by a narrow margin, she would have ordered D to pay P's costs to the date of the payment in and thereafter that P should pay D's costs. The Court of Appeal *held* that this was a wrong approach as it involved a double penalty on P which was the succesful party: on this approach P would have failed to obtain its own costs and additionally would have to pay those of the losing party. The just result was

---

[1] paras 2.2, 11.1 and 11.5.
[2] (1997) C.A.T. 1363; [1997] C.L.Y. 555.

that P should have its costs to the date of the payment in and that thereafter there should be no order as to costs. Of this result, it was said—

per Evans L.J.: "Where the plaintiff recovers more than the amount of the payment in, the defendant cannot say that the plaintiff has failed to beat it, and claim an order in his favour on that ground. But the Court can say to both parties, where the defendant has made a payment in but without admitting that that sum was due, 'You have each tried for a higher or a lower figure, and in practical terms neither of you has succeeded. You should each pay your own costs of the Court time you have used'."

per Swinton Thomas L.J.: ". . . the basic rule [is] that costs follow the event and . . . a Plaintiff who recovers more than the payment in will recover his costs unless there are special circumstances or it appears to the court that some different order should be made. There remains a discretion which must be exercised judicially but the courts are not tied in a mathematical straight jacket. In this case the Plaintiff has . . . beaten the payment in by a few thousand dollars. On the facts of this case . . . any reasonable bystander or onlooker, if told that the Plaintiff had recovered a few thousand dollars more than [it] had been offered well before the trial began, would . . . take the view that the Plaintiff should pay the costs incurred since the date the offer was made." However, in the circumstances of this case, bearing in mind that "the [Plaintiff was] clearly at fault in that [it] should have accepted the sum . . . offered" and that "the Defendants were at fault in not paying into court the amount that was eventually recovered by the [Plaintiff], abroad justice can be achieved between the parties . . . by ordering that the Defendants pay the Plaintiff's costs to the date of the payment into court, and that each party should bear its own costs thereafter."

12.3 The final result in relation to costs in the foregoing case is hardly surprising: to spend 30 days of very expensive time to obtain two per cent more than had previously been offered in the context of what, on the trial judge's findings, was a vastly exaggerated claim was clearly disproportionate. The facts of the case were stark and are unlikely to be replicated, even closely, with any great frequency. However, the greater flexibility likely to be adopted by the courts in relation to costs under the new rules may mean that close attention will be paid to the cost of achieving only a fairly small advance on what had previously been offered. Disproportionate costs in achieving only a marginal improvement on a Part 36 offer or Part 36 payment may make it appropriate for the general rule to be modified.[3] Whilst the circumstances of every such case would vary, an order in the nature of that made in the *Charm Maritime* case would often do broad justice to the situation.

12.4 If the court is prepared to entertain the kind of argument foreshadowed above in relation to a narrow victory for a claimant, is there scope for a similar argument on the part of a claimant who narrowly fails to achieve

---

[3] para. 2.2, above. In the type of situation considered in the text, it would be open to the offeror, whose offer or Part 36 payment had been beaten, but only just, to invite the court to exercise its discretion to make "a different order" from the normal order: r. 44.3(2)(b). The provisions of r. 44.3(4) and (5) would need to be applied in considering the offeror's argument. The court will doubtless have in mind its powers under r. 44.3(6) in this context. *cf. Re Elgindata (No. 2)* [1992] 1 W.L.R. 1207, CA.

what had previously been offered? There is no doubt that the discretion to modify the normal rule exists.[4] There may well be cases where the court would be tempted to try to ameliorate the consequences of the normal result of failure to better an offer or Part 36 payment. A situation where the court is likely to be concerned would be where a severely disabled claimant "misses" a Part 36 payment by only a very modest amount and the result of the normal costs order would be to reduce or even obliterate desperately needed compensation. It remains to be seen whether the greater flexibility of the new rules will permit this kind of argument to be advanced successfully.[5] The difficulty lying in the way of permitting it to succeed is that the defendant who has successfully judged the likely award of the court and who has made its arrangements around that judgment will suffer a financial penalty. Indeed defendants may question whether there is much purpose in making a Part 36 payment at all. Furthermore, any latitude given to a claimant in this kind of situation may encourage others not to address a reasonable offer with suitable care. The objective of early settlement on reasonable terms will be frustrated if too much benevolence is shown.

The jurisdiction to depart from the normal rule in either of the two **12.5** situations referred to above plainly exists. It is, however, suggested that it would only be in very exceptional circumstances that any significant departure from the normal or general rule would be entertained.

---

[4] para. 11.6, above.
[5] But see *Abada v. Gray and anor*, referred to in n.24, Chap. 11.

CHAPTER 13

Miscellaneous matters relating to Part 36

Introduction

13.1 This Chapter deals with a number of miscellaneous matters arising from Part 36. Merely because each can be dealt with quite shortly does not mean that these matters are not important.

Part 20 claims

13.2 Any claim other than one made by a claimant against a defendant is known as a "Part 20 claim". It includes a counterclaim by a defendant against the claimant or some other party, a claim by a defendant against any person (whether or not already a party) for contribution, indemnity or some other relief, and a claim made by someone against whom a Part 20 claim has been made.[1] A Part 20 claim is treated by the rules as if it were a claim[2] and, accordingly, Part 36 applies to any such claim.

13.3 The effect of these provisions is to make it incumbent on a defendant to a Part 20 claim in which there is a money claim to make a Part 36 payment if he wishes to protect his position in relation to costs.[3] A claim by an original defendant against another party for an indemnity or contribution in relation to a money claim brought against him would seem to be a money claim in its own right. On that basis, in general terms, a Part 36 payment would need to be made to ensure protection on costs. However, the defendant to the Part 20 claim may be in some difficulty in doing this. He may, for example, be prepared to contribute to, say, 50 per cent of the

---

[1] r.20.2(1).
[2] r.20.3(1).
[3] r.36.3(1).

60

claimant's claim, but may have a different view as to the quantum of that claim than the view formed by the original defendant to that claim. That would make the assessment of what sum to pay into court very difficult. The sum paid in could be accepted by the original defendant who then either negotiates a settlement with the claimant, or secures a judgment from the court, in a sum less than the assessment of quantum made by the defendant to the Part 20 claim. If the Part 20 defendant is prepared to take that risk, then there is no problem in making a Part 36 payment. If, on the other hand, he wishes merely to offer a proportion of the claimant's claim without making a payment into court,[4] it is likely that the purposive construction to be given to the rules[5] and the overall flexibility within Part 36,[6] ought to allow such an offer to be made and to be effective on the question of costs.

13.4 A defendant to a Part 20 claim who is thereafter joined as a defendant to the principal claim can, of course, make a Part 36 payment against the original claimant's claim. If accepted by that claimant, that will end the dispute between them, although the original defendant may still be able to pursue a claim for a further contribution from the defendant who has settled with the claimant, but who remains a defendant to the Part 20 claim.[7]

Small claims

13.5 Because of the limited costs provisions in relation to cases on the small claims track,[8] Part 36 does not apply to small claims cases.[9] Rule 36.2(5) provides that a Part 36 offer or a Part 36 payment "shall not have the consequences set out in this Part while the claim is being dealt with on the small claims track unless the court orders otherwise."

13.6 The foregoing provision is not designed to discourage offers of settlement, or payments into court, in relation to small claims cases. It merely provides that the automatic consequences of a Part 36 offer or Part 36 payment will not apply whilst a claim is on a small claims track. The proviso that the court may order otherwise is designed to enable the court to make a suitable order where, for example, a defendant has spent a considerable amount of money in costs in relation to an inflated claim which is subsequently reduced and transferred to the small claims track.[10]

---

[4] Which is permitted in non-money claims: r.36.5(4).
[5] r.1.2(b).
[6] r.36.1(2).
[7] cf. *Harper v. Gray and Walker* [1985] 1 W.L.R. 1196.
[8] r.27.14(2), (3) and (4).
[9] r.27.2(1)(g).
[10] para. 4.8, Minutes of the Civil Procedure Rules Committee meeting, September 17, 1998.

Provisional damages

13.7 Where a defendant faces a claim which includes a claim for provisional damages, he has two options: he can either make a Part 36 payment without offering to agree to an award of provisional damages or he can make a Part 36 payment and at the same time specify whether he will agree to an award of provisional damages.[11] When he chooses the latter course, his Part 36 payment notice[12] must so specify.[13] He must also give the appropriate details required by the rules so that the claimant will know the basis of the offer.[14]

13.8 Where the defendant makes a Part 36 payment and offers to agree to a provisional damages award, and the claimant gives notice of acceptance within the usual 21-day period, the normal costs consequences[15] will result unless the court orders otherwise.[16]

13.9 If the claimant accepts the Part 36 payment on the basis offered, he must apply to the court within seven days of doing so for an order for an award of provisional damages.[17] If the court makes the award,[18] the money in court will be paid out.[19]

Converting an ordered payment into court to a Part 36 payment

13.10 A party may be ordered to pay money into court under the rules for various reasons.[20] Where that happens, the party may convert that enforced payment into court into a Part 36 payment if he wishes to do so. All that he needs to do is to file a Part 36 payment notice in accordance

---

[11] r.36.7(1) and (2).
[12] Chaps 4 and 6.
[13] r.36.7(2).
[14] r.36.7(3).
[15] para. 9.4, above.
[16] r.36.7(4).
[17] Part 41 provides the machinery whereby this application is made.
[18] Since an award of provisional damages is, strictly speaking, a discretionary matter (*Willson v. Ministry of Defence* [1991] 1 All E.R. 638), the court could theoretically decline to make an award notwithstanding the agreement of the parties. However, this would be a very unusual course to adopt.
[19] r.36.7(6).
[20] Under Part 24 the court can make a conditional order on a summary judgment application requiring the defendant to pay a sum of money into court: Part 24 Practice Direction, para. 5. Further, under the general powers of case management, the court can order the payment of a sum of money into court: r.3.1(3) and (5). Although r.37.2(1) says that where a defendant makes a payment into court "following an order made under r.3.1(3) or 3.1(5) he may choose to treat the whole or any part of the money paid into court as a Part 36 payment", it is not thought that the intention was to restrict the ability to convert a payment into court solely to payments into court made under the rules thus specified.

with r.36.6.[21] The court will serve it unless he notifies the court at the time of filing the Part 36 payment notice that he intends to do so.[22]

Apportionment of money accepted in settlement of a Fatal Accidents Act claim

The rules require the apportionment of a single sum of money paid into **13.11** court in satisfaction of claims under the Fatal Accidents Act and the Law Reform (Miscellaneous Provisions) Act 1934 between the two claims.[23] The same requirement applies in relation to the claims of dependants under the Fatal Accidents Act (1976).[24]

Transitional arrangements

The general scheme of the Transitional Arrangements is to apply the Civil **13.12** Procedure Rules with effect from April 26, 1999 "to defended cases so far as practicable".[25] This scheme finds expression in the Practice Direction concerning Transitional Arrangements. Specific provision is made to the effect that where a party "has taken any step in the proceedings in accordance with the previous rules that step will remain valid on or after April 26, 1999".[26] This means that any payment into court made prior to that date (and indeed any other offer of settlement made in accordance with the previous rules[27]) will be "valid". It is submitted that this means that it is fully effective within the previous rules and (a) can be accepted in accordance with those rules and (b) will be managed or otherwise evaluated in accordance with the practice under those rules.

---

[21] r.37.2(2) and Part 37 Practice Direction, para. 3.2.
[22] r.36.6(3).
[23] r.37.4(1).
[24] r.37.4(3).
[25] Part 51 Practice Direction, para. 2(b).
[26] *ibid.*, para. 10(1).
[27] See para. 3.1, above.

CHAPTER 14

Obtaining a consent order under the new rules

The phraseology of a consent order or judgment

14.1 The new rules have not changed the substantive law relating to compromise. A compromise is a contract which, if embodied in a consent order or judgment, has a dual personality: it remains a contract, but has the added status and authority conferred by the court order.

14.2 One fundamental proposition of law, which finds its reflection in long-established court practice, is that the parties cannot by consent confer upon the court a jurisdiction that it does not otherwise possess.[1] It follows that parties who do wish to embody their agreement in a court order that is enforceable must do so in a way that does not offend this proposition. This requires them to draw up a consent order that comes fairly within the jurisdiction of the court. It is sensible practice, therefore, to utilise the wording of any established form of order or judgment for the purposes of drawing up an agreed order. Since the enforcement provisions under the former rules effectively remain in force for the time being, no significant changes in the approach to drafting final consent orders or judgments will need to be made yet.[2]

14.3 Notwithstanding the absence of the expression "Tomlin order" in the new rules,[3] the Tomlin order will still be the principal method by which is concluded a compromise involving terms going beyond the normal jurisdiction of the court.[4] Since a Tomlin order drafted after April 26, 1999 will need to reflect the language of the new rules, some modification of the traditional formulation of such an order may be thought inevitable.[5]

---

[1] Foskett, *op cit.*, para. 15–12 *et seq* and para. 16–06 *et seq.*
[2] If discontinuance is the mechanism by which a compromise is concluded (which would be rare), regard should be had to Part 38.
[3] Chap. 9, n.44.
[4] Foskett, *op cit.*, para. 15–14 *et seq.*
[5] See Appendix VII.

The practice of obtaining a consent order or judgment

The practice in relation to the obtaining by the parties of a consent order **14.4** or judgment has hardly changed from that obtaining hitherto. Where the proposed consent order or judgment is one of a number of fairly straightforward forms provided for in the rules,[6] and provided that none of the parties is a litigant in person, nor is the approval of the court as such to the order required, a court officer may enter and seal the order.[7] If this procedure is followed, the order or judgment will not bear the name and judicial title of the person who made it[8] because, of course, it will not have received any judicial scrutiny and will not have received any judicial authority as such. The order will, however, have the full authority of the court.

Where the foregoing procedure is adopted, the court officer will be **14.5** concerned to ensure that the proposed order falls fairly and squarely within the terms of rule 40.6(3). If there is any doubt, he will refer the order to the master, district judge or judge. It will also be of concern to the court officer to ensure that none of the parties is a litigant in person. The purported making of an order pursuant to this procedure when one of the parties is a litigant in person would undoubtedly invalidate the order.[9] Where a represented party agrees a proposed consent order with a litigant in person, it would be prudent for the solicitor drawing up the order for submission to the court to write a covering letter to the court stating expressly that rule 40.6(3) does *not* apply. This should ensure that judicial scrutiny is given to the order. The fact that it has been presented to a master, district judge or judge should be checked when the order is returned by the court.[10]

When the provisions of rule 40.6(2) and (3) do not apply, an application to **14.6** the court should be made.[11] The application, which will usually be dealt with by a master or district judge, can be dealt with without a hearing.[12] All applications are governed by Part 23. Since all parties are agreed that the particular consent order should be made, it is likely that the application will be made without serving an application notice.[13] The agreed order

---

[6] r.40.6(3). It will be noted that (b)(ii) refers to an order for "the stay of proceedings on agreed terms, disposing of the proceedings, whether those terms are recorded in a schedule to the order or elsewhere". This is intended to refer to a Tomlin order. The words "or elsewhere" were inserted to cater for the situation in which the parties (as they do with increasing frequency) wish to record the substance of their agreement other than in the schedule to the order (which is part of the court record and open for inspection) and thus keep it confidential: Foskett, *op cit.*, para. 16–19.

[7] r.40.6(2).

[8] r.40.2(1)(c).

[9] *National Westminster Bank Plc v. Smillie*, QBD, February 4, 1999.

[10] *ibid.*

[11] r.40.6(5).

[12] r.40.6(6); r.23.8(a).

[13] Part 23 Practice Direction, para. 3(3).

must be drawn up in the agreed terms, be expressed to be "by consent" and be signed by the legal representative acting for each party to whom the order relates or by the party if he is a litigant in person.[14] Where all parties affected by the order have written to the court consenting to the making of the order, a draft of which has been filed with the court, the draft will be treated as having been signed by all parties.[15] So far as litigants in person are concerned, the practice hitherto has been for the court to accept a consent order signed by a litigant in person when it is satisfied that the signature is genuine and that the consent is also genuine and voluntarily given.[16] That practice is likely to continue. The master or district judge would be entitled to ask the litigant in person to attend before him, or to ask for some second written confirmation of agreement, if he had any reservations about the matter.

Information required by court

14.7 The Part 23 Practice Direction places upon the parties who wish to follow the procedures available in rule 40.6 the onus of ensuring that the court is provided "with any material it needs to be satisfied that it is appropriate to make the order."[17] This might include, for example, reference to some particular authority or statutory provision so as to demonstrate that the court does have jurisdiction to make a particular order which, at first sight, might seem unusual.

Settlements reached just before or during trial

14.8 Where a settlement is not reached until just before or during the trial, the current practice is likely to continue. On the basis that no approval as such is required from the court, an appropriate consent order or judgment will be agreed between the parties which the trial judge will be invited to make. If approval is needed, the trial judge will be invited to give that approval.

Settlements requiring the approval of the court

14.9 A settlement involving a child or patient may be concluded prior to the commencement of proceedings. If so, the approval of the court will still be required for the agreement to be binding. The Part 21 Practice Direction

---

[14] r.40.7.
[15] Part 23 Practice Direction, para. 10.2.
[16] *Supreme Court Practice 1999*, vol. 2, para. 17A–31.
[17] Practice Direction, para. 10.4. A letter is usually acceptable for this purpose.

sets out the procedure to be adopted[18] and the information required. The Practice Direction deals with the information required when the settlement is of a claim arising from an accident. The information may need to be amplified where the claim arose out of alleged clinical negligence. For example, an issue which frequently arises in that context is that of causation. The defence may accept the alleged negligence (either in whole or in part), but denies that it caused or materially contributed to the condition of which complaint is made. Where the claimant is prepared to make a discount to reflect the risks of an adverse finding concerning this, the court will need to be informed about this and about how the claimant's advisers see the issue.

14.10 Where counsel has advised on the settlement, it is normal for counsel's opinion to be placed before the court.

14.11 Where the settlement is concluded after the institution of proceedings, an application for approval will have to be made. If the settlement is concluded well before the trial, the application can be dealt with by the master or district judge under rule 40.6. In cases of difficulty, the application might be referred to a judge. If the settlement is achieved at or shortly before trial, the approval will doubtless be sought from the trial judge.

Notification of settlement to court

14.12 Where a settlement is reached which disposes of the whole claim for which a date or "window" has been fixed for trial, the parties must notify the listing officer for the trial court immediately.[19] Where a sealed order giving effect to the settlement has been obtained, a copy of the sealed order should be filed with the listing officer.[20]

---

[18] Paras 6.1–6.3: Appendix IV.
[19] Part 39 Practice Direction, para. 4.1.
[20] *ibid.*, para. 4.2.

APPENDIX I

Part 36

OFFERS TO SETTLE AND PAYMENTS INTO COURT

CONTENTS OF THIS PART

Scope of this part

15.1   36.1 — (1) This Part containes rules about—

    (a) offers to settle and payments into court; and
    (b) the consequences where an offer to settle or payment into court is made in accordance with this Part.

(2) Nothing in this Part prevents a party making an offer to settle in whatever way he chooses, but if that offer is not made in accordance with this Part, it will have the consequences specified in this Part if the court so orders.
(Part 36 applies to part 20 claims by virtue of rule 20.3).

Part 36 offers and Part 36 payments — general provisions

15.2   36.2 — (1) An offer made in accordance with the requirements of this Part is called—

    (a) if made by way of a payment into court, 'a Part 36 payment';
    (b) otherwise 'a Part 36 offer'.

(Rule 36.3 sets out when an offer has to be made by way of a payment into court).

(2) The party who makes an offer is the 'offeror'.
(3) The party to whom an offer is made is the 'offeree'.
(4) A Part 36 offer or a Part 36 payment—

    (a) may be made at any time after proceedings have started; and
    (b) may be made in appeal proceedings.

(5) A Part 36 offer or a Part 36 payment shall not have the consequences set out in this Part while the claim is being dealt with on the small claims track unless the court orders otherwise.

(Part 26 deals with allocation to the small claims track)
(Rule 27.2 provides that Part 36 does not apply to small claims)

A defendant's offer to settle a money claim requires a Part 36 payment

15.3   36.3 — (1) Subject to rules 36.5(5) and 36.23, an offer by a defendant to settle a money claim will not have the consequences set out in this Part unless it is made by way of a Part 36 payment.
(2) A Part 36 payment may only be made after proceedings have started.

(Rule 36.5(5) permits a Part 36 offer to be made by reference to an interim payment)

(Rule 36.10 makes provision for an offer to settle a money claim before the commencement of proceedings)

(Rule 36.23 makes provision for where benefit is recoverable under the Social Security (Recovery of Benefit) Act 1997[1])

Defendant's offer to settle the whole of a claim which includes both a money claim and a non-money claim

36.4 — (1) This rule applies where a defendant to a claim which includes both a   **15.4**
money claim and a non-money claim wishes—

    (a) to make an offer to settle the whole claim which will have the consequences set out in this Part; and

    (b) to make a money offer in respect of the money claim and a non-money offer in respect of the non-money claim.[2]

(2) The defendant must—

    (a) make a Part 36 payment in relation to the money claim; and

    (b) make a Part 36 offer in relation to the non-money claim.

(3) The Part 36 payment notice must—

    (a) identify the document which sets out the terms of the Part 36 offer; and

    (b) state that if the claimant gives notice of acceptance of the Part 36 payment he will be treated as also accepting the Part 36 offer.

(Rule 36.6 makes provision for a Part 36 payment notice)

(4) If the claimant gives notice of acceptance of the Part 36 payment, he shall also be taken as giving notice of acceptance of the Part 36 offer in relation to the non-money claim.

Form and content of a Part 36 offer

36.5 — (1) A Part 36 offer must be in writing.   **15.5**

(2) A Part 36 offer may relate to the whole claim or to part of it or to any issue that arises in it.

(3) A Part 36 offer must—

    (a) state whether it relates to the whole of the claim or to part of it or to an issue that arises in it and if so to which part or issue;

    (b) state whether it takes into account any counterclaim; and

    (c) if it is expressed not to be inclusive of interest, give the details relating to interest set out in rule 36.22(2).

---

[1] 1997 c.27.

[2] Inserted by Civil Procedure (Amendment) Rules 1999.

(4) A defendant may make a Part 36 offer limited to accepting liability up to a specified proportion.

(5) A Part 36 offer may be made by reference to an interim payment.

(Part 25 contains provisions relating to interim payments)

(6) A Part 36 offer made not less than 21 days before the start of the trial must—

    (a) be expressed to remain open for acceptance for 21 days from the date it is made; and

    (b) provide that after 21 days the offeree may only accept it if—

        (i) the parties agree the liability for costs; or

        (ii) the court gives permission.

(7) A Part 36 offer made less than 21 days before the start of the trial must state that the offeree may only accept it if—

    (a) the parties agree the liability for costs; or

    (b) the court gives permission.

(Rule 36.8 makes provision for when a Part 36 offer is treated as being made)

(8) If a Part 36 offer is withdrawn it will not have the consequences set out in this Part.

Notice of a Part 36 payment

15.6   **36.6** — (1) A Part 36 payment may relate to the whole claim or part of it or to an issue that arises in it.

(2) A defendant who makes a Part 36 payment must file with the court a notice ('Part 36 payment notice') which—

    (a) states the amount of the payment;

    (b) states whether the payment relates to the whole claim or to part of it or to any issue that arises in it and if so to which part or issue;

    (c) states whether it takes into account any counterclaim;

    (d) if an interim payment has been made, states that the defendant has taken into account the interim payment; and

    (e) if it is expressed not to be inclusive of interest, gives the details relating to interest set out in rule 36.22(2).

(Rule 25.6 makes provisions for an interim payment)

(Rule 36.4 provides for further information to be included where a defendant wishes to settle the whole of a claim which includes a money claim and a non-money claim)

(Rule 36.23 makes provision for extra information to be included in the payment notice in a case where benefit is recoverable under the Social Security (Recovery of Benefit) Act 1997)

(3) The court will serve the Part 36 payment notice on the offeree unless the offeror informs the court, when the money is paid into court, that the offeror will serve the notice.[3]

---

[3] Words inserted by Civil Procedure (Amendment) Rules 1999.

(4) Where the offeror serves the Part 36 payment notice he must file a certificate of service.

(Rule 6.10 specifies what must be contained in a certificate of service)

(5) A Part 36 payment may be withdrawn only with the permission of the court.

Offer to settle a claim for provisional damages

36.7 — (1) A defendant may make a Part 36 payment in respect of a claim **15.7** which includes a claim for provisional damages.

(2) Where he does so, the Part 36 payment notice must specify whether or not the defendant is offering to agree to the making of an award of provisional damages.

(3) Where the defendant is offering to agree to the making of an award of provisional damages the payment notice must also state—

(a) that the sum paid into court is in satisfaction of the claim for damages on the assumption that the injured person will not develop the disease or suffer the type of deterioration specified in the notice;

(b) that the offer is subject to the condition that the claimant must make any claim for further damages within a limited period; and

(c) what that period is.

(4) Where a Part 36 payment is—

(a) made in accordance with paragraph (3); and

(b) accepted within the relevant period in rule 36.11,

the Part 36 payment will have the consequences set out in rule 36.13, unless the court orders otherwise.

(5) If the claimant accepts the Part 36 payment he must, within 7 days of doing so, apply to the court for an order for an award of provisional damage under rule 41.2.

(Rule 41.2 provides for an order for an award of provisional damages)

(6) The money in court may not be paid out until the court has disposed of the application made in accordance with paragraph (5).

Time when a Part 36 offer or a Part 36 payment is made and accepted

36.8 — (1) A Part 36 offer is made when received by the offeree. **15.8**

(2) A Part 36 payment is made when written notice of the payment into court is served on the offeree.

(3) An improvement to a Part 36 offer will be effective when its details are received by the offeree.

(4) An increase in a Part 36 payment will be effective when notice of the increase is served on the offeree.

(5) A Part 36 offer or Part 36 payment is accepted when notice of its acceptance is received by the offeror.

Clarification of a Part 36 offer or a Part 36 payment notice

15.9   36.9 — (1) The offeree may, within 7 days of a Part 36 offer or payment being made, request the offeror to clarify the offer or payment notice.

(2) If the offeror does not give the clarification requested under paragraph (1) within 7 days of receiving the request, the offeree may, unless the trial has started, apply for an order that he does so.

(3) If the court makes an order under paragraph (2), it must specify the date when the Part 36 offer or Part 36 payment is to be treated as having been made.

Court to take into account offer to settle made before commencement of proceedings

15.10   36.10 — (1) If a person makes an offer to settle before proceedings are begun which complies with the provisions of this rule, the court will take that offer into account when making any order as to costs.

(2) The offer must—

    (a) be expressed to be open for at least 21 days after the date it was made;

    (b) if made by a person who would be a defendant were proceedings commenced, include an offer to pay the costs of the offeree incurred up to the date 21 days after the date it was made; and

    (c) otherwise comply with this Part.

(3) If the offeror is a defendant to a money claim—

    (a) he must make a Part 36 payment within 14 days of service of the claim form; and

    (b) the amount of the payment must be not less than the sum offered before proceedings began.

(4) An offeree may not, after proceedings have begun, accept—

    (a) an offer made under paragraph (2); or

    (b) a Part 36 payment made under paragraph (3), without the permission of the court.

(5) An offer under this rule is made when it is received by the offeree.

Time for acceptance of a defendant's Part 36 offer or Part 36 payment

15.11   36.11 — (1) A claimant may accept a Part 36 offer or a Part 36 payment made not less than 21 days before the start of the trial without needing the court's permission if he gives the defendant written notice of acceptance not later than 21 days after the offer or payment was made.

(Rule 36.13 sets out the costs consequences of accepting a defendant's offer or payment without needing the permission of the court)

(2) If—

(a) a defendant's Part 36 offer or Part 36 payment is made less than 21 days before the start of the trial; or

(b) the claimant does not accept it within the period specified in paragraph (1)—

(i) if the parties agree the liability for costs, the claimant may accept the offer or payment without needing the permission of the court;

(ii) if the parties do not agree the liability for costs the claimant may only accept the offer or payment with the permission of the court.

(3) Where the permission of the court is needed under paragraph (2) the court will, if it gives permission, make an order as to costs.

Time for acceptance of a claimant's Part 36 offer

36.12 — (1) A defendant may accept a Part 36 offer made not less than 21 days **15.12** before the start of the trial without needing the court's permission if he gives the claimant written notice of acceptance not later than 21 days after the offer was made.

(Rule 36.14 sets out the costs consequences of accepting a claimant's offer without needing the permission of the court)

(2) If—

(a) a claimant's Part 36 offer is made less than 21 days before the start of the trial; or

(b) the defendant does not accept it within the period specified in paragraph (1)—

(i) if the parties agree the liability for costs, the defendant may accept the offer without needing the permission of the court;

(ii) if the parties do not agree the liability for costs the defendant may only accept the offer with the permission of the court.

(3) Where the permission of the court is needed under paragraph (2) the court will, if it gives permission, makes an order as to costs.

Costs consequences of acceptance of a defendant's Part 36 offer or Part 36 payment

36.13 — (1) Where a Part 36 offer or a Part 36 payment is accepted without **15.13** needing the permission of the court the claimant will be entitled to his costs of the proceedings up to the date of serving notice of acceptance.

(2) Where—

(a) a Part 36 offer or a Part 36 payment relates to part only of the claim; and

(b) at the time of serving notice of acceptance the claimant abandons the balance of the claim,

the claimant will be entitled to his costs of the proceedings up to the date of serving notice of acceptance, unless the court orders otherwise.

(3) The claimant's costs include any costs attributable to the defendant's counterclaim if the Part 36 offer or the Part 36 payment notice states that it takes into account the counterclaim.

(4) Costs under this rule will be payable on the standard basis if not agreed.

Costs consequences of acceptance of a claimant's Part 36 offer

15.14   36.14 — Where a claimant's Part 36 offer is accepted without needing the permission of the court the claimant will be entitled to his costs of the proceedings up to the date upon which the defendant serves notice of acceptance.

The effect of acceptance of a Part 36 offer or a Part 36 payment

15.15   36.15 — (1) If a Part 36 offer or Part 36 payment relates to the whole claim and is accepted, the claim will be stayed(GL).

(2) In the case of acceptance of a Part 36 offer which relates to the whole claim—

(a) the stay(GL) will be upon the terms of the offer; and

(b) either party may apply to enforce those terms without the need for a new claim.

(3) If a Part 36 offer or a Part 36 payment which relates to part only of the claim is accepted—

(a) the claim will be stayed(GL) as to that part; and

(b) unless the parties have agreed costs, the liability for costs shall be decided by the court.

(4) If the approval of the court is required before a settlement can be binding, any stay(GL) which would otherwise arise on the acceptance of a Part 36 offer or a Part 36 payment will take effect only when that approval has been given.

(5) Any stay(GL) arising under this rule will not affect the power of the court—

(a) to enforce the terms of a Part 36 offer;

(b) to deal with any question of costs (including interest on costs) relating to the proceedings;

(c) to order payment out of court of any sum paid into court.

(6) Where—

(a) a Part 36 offer has been accepted; and
(b) a party alleges that—

> (i) the other party has not honoured the terms of the offer; and
> (ii) he is therefore entitled to a remedy for breach of contract,

the party may claim the remedy by applying to the court without the need to start a new claim unless the court orders otherwise.

Payment out of a sum in court on the acceptance of a Part 36 payment

36.16 — Where a Part 36 payment is accepted the claimant obtains payment out **15.16** of the sum in court by making a request for payment in the practice form.

Acceptance of a Part 36 offer or a Part 36 payment made by one or more, but not all, defendants

36.17 — (1) This rule applies where the claimant wishes to accept a Part 36 **15.17** offer or a Part 36 payment made by one or more, but not all, of a number of defendants.

(2) If the defendants are sued jointly or in the alternative, the claimant may accept the offer or payment without needing the permission of the court in accordance with rule 36.11(1) if—

(a) he discontinues his claim against those defendants who have not made the offer or payment; and
(b) those defendants give written consent to the acceptance of the offer or payment.

(3) If the claimant alleges that the defendants have a several liability$^{(GL)}$ to him the claimant may—

(a) accept the offer or payment in accordance with rule 36.11(1); and
(b) continue with his claims against the other defendants if he is entitled to do so.[4]

(4) In all other cases the claimant must apply to the court for—

(a) an order permitting a payment out to him of any sum in court; and
(b) such order as to costs as the court considers appropriate.

Other cases where a court order is required to enable acceptance of a Part 36 offer or a Part 36 payment

36.18 — (1) Where a Part 36 offer or a Part 36 payment is made in proceedings **15.18** to which rule 21.10 applies—

---

[4] Words inserted by Civil Procedure (Amendment) Rules 1999.

    (a) the offer or payment may be accepted only with the permission of the court; and

    (b) no payment out of any sum in court shall be made without a court order.

(Rule 21.10 deals with compromise etc. by or on behalf of a child or patient)

(2) Where the court gives a claimant permission to accept a Part 36 offer or payment after the trial has started—

    (a) any money in court may be paid out only with a court order; and

    (b) the court must, in the order, deal with the whole costs of the proceedings.

(3) Where a claimant accepts a Part 36 payment after a defence of tender before claim$^{(GL)}$ has been put forward by the defendant, the money in court may be paid out only after an order of the court.

(Rule 37.3 requires a defendant who wishes to rely on a defence of tender before claim$^{(GL)}$ to make a payment into court)

Restriction on disclosure of a Part 36 offer or a Part 36 payment

15.19   36.19 — (1) A Part 36 offer will be treated as 'without prejudice$^{(GL)}$ except as to costs'.

(2) The fact that a Part 36 payment has been made shall not be communicated to the trial judge until all questions of liability and the amount of money to be awarded have been decided.

(3) Paragraph (2) does not apply—

    (a) where the defence of tender before claim$^{(GL)}$ has been raised;

    (b) where the proceedings have been stayed$^{(GL)}$ under rule 36.15 following acceptance of a Part 36 offer or Part 36 payment; or

    (c) where—

       (i) the issue of liability has been determined before any assessment of the money claimed; and

       (ii) the fact that there has or has not been a Part 36 payment may be relevant to the question of the costs of the issue of liability.

Costs consequences where claimant fails to do better than a Part 36 offer or a Part 36 payment

15.20   36.20 — (1) This rule applies where at trial a claimant—

    (a) fails to better a Part 36 payment; or

    (b) fails to obtain a judgment which is more advantageous than a Part 36 offer.

(2) Unless it considers it unjust to do so, the court will order the claimant to pay any costs incurred by the defendant after the latest date on which the payment or offer could have been accepted without needing the permission of the court.

(Rule 36.11 sets out the time for acceptance of a defendant's Part 36 offer or Part 36 payment)

Costs and other consequences where claimant does better than he proposed in his Part 36 offer

36.21 — (1) This rule applies where at trial—
15.21

    (a) a defendant is held liable for more; or
    (b) the judgment against a defendant is more advantageous to the claimant,

than the proposals contained in a claimant's Part 36 offer.

(2) The court may order interest on the whole or part of any sum of money (excluding interest) awarded to the claimant at a rate not exceeding 10 per cent above base rate(GL) for some or all of the period starting with the latest date on which the defendant could have accepted the offer without needing the permission of the court.

(3) The court may also order that the claimant is entitled to—

    (a) his costs on the indemnity basis from the latest date when the defendant could have accepted the offer without needing the permission of the court; and
    (b) interest on those costs at a rate not exceeding 10 per cent above base rate(GL).

(4) Where this rule applies, the court will make the orders referred to in paragraph (2) and (3) unless it considers it unjust to do so.

(Rule 36.12 sets out the latest date when the defendant could have accepted the offer)

(5) In considering whether it would be unjust to make the orders referred to in paragraphs (2) and (3) above, the court will take into account all the circumstances of the case including—

    (a) the terms of any Part 36 offer;
    (b) the stage in the proceedings when any Part 36 offer or Part 36 payment was made;
    (c) the information available to the parties at the time when the Part 36 offer or Part 36 payment was made; and
    (d) the conduct of the parties with regard to the giving or refusing to give information for the purposes of enabling the offer or payment into court to be made or evaluated.

(6) The power of the court under this rule is in addition to any other power it may have to award interest.

Interest

15.22   36.22 — (1) Unless—

(a) a claimant's Part 36 offer which offers to accept a sum of money; or
(b) a Part 36 payment notice,

indicates to the contrary, any such offer or payment will be treated as inclusive of all interest until the last date on which it could be accepted without needing the permission of the court.

(2) Where a claimant's Part 36 offer or Part 36 payment notice is expressed not to be inclusive of interest, the offer or notice must state—

(a) whether interest is offered; and
(b) if so, the amount offered, the rate or rates offered and the period or periods for which it is offered.

Deduction of benefits

15.23   36.23 — (1) This rule applies where a payment to a claimant following acceptance of a Part 36 offer or Part 36 payment into court would be a compensation payment as defined in section 1 of the Social Security (Recovery of Benefits) Act 1997.[5]

(2) A defendant to a money claim may make an offer to settle the claim which will have the consequences set out in this Part, without making a Part 36 payment if—

(a) at the time he makes the offer he has applied for, but not received, a certificate of recoverable benefit; and
(b) he makes a Part 36 payment not more than 7 days after he receives the certificate.

(Section 1 of the 1997 Act defines 'recoverable benefit')

(3) A Part 36 payment notice must state—

(a) the amount of gross compensation;
(b) the name and amount of any benefit by which that gross amount is reduced in accordance with section 8 and Schedule 2 to the 1997 Act; and
(c) that the sum paid in is the net amount after deduction of the amount of benefit.

(4) For the purposes of rule 36.20, a claimant fails to better a Part 36 payment if he fails to obtain judgment for more than the gross sum specified in the Part 36 payment notice.

---

[5] 1997 c.27.

(5) Where—

    (a) a Part 36 payment has been made; and
    (b) application is made for the money remaining in court to be paid out,

the court may treat the money in court as being reduced by a sum equivalent to any further recoverable benefits paid to the claimant since the date of payment into court and may direct payment out accordingly.

APPENDIX II

Practice Direction — Offers to settle and payments into court

THIS PRACTICE DIRECTION SUPPLEMENTS CPR PART 36

Part 36 offers and Part 36 payments

16.1   1.1 A written offer to settle a claim[1] or part of a claim or any issue that arises in it made in accordance with the provisions of Part 36 is called:

(1) if made by way of a payment into court, a Part 36 payment,[2] or
(2) if made otherwise, a Part 36 offer.[3]

1.2 A Part 36 offer or Part 36 payment has the costs and other consequences set out in rules 36.13, 36.14, 36.20 and 36.21.

1.3 An offer to settle which is not made in accordance with Part 36 will only have the consequences specified in that Part if the court so orders and will be given such weight on any issue as to costs as the court thinks appropriate.[4]

Parties and Part 36 offers

16.2   2.1 A Part 36 offer, subject to paragraph 3 below, may be made by any party.

2.2 The party making an offer is the 'offeror' and the party to whom it is made is the 'offeree'.

2.3 A Part 36 offer may consist of a proposal to settle for a specified sum or for some other remedy.

---

[1] Includes Part 20 claims.
[2] See r.36.2(1)(a).
[3] See r.36.2(1)(b).
[4] See r.36.1(2).

2.4 A Part 36 offer is made when received by the offeree.[5]

2.5 An improvement to a Part 36 offer is effective when its details are received by the offeree.[6]

Parties and Part 36 payments

3.1 An offer to settle for a specified sum made by a defendant[7] must, in order to comply with Part 36, be made by way of a Part 36 payment into court.[8]   **16.3**

3.2 A Part 36 payment is made when the Part 36 payment notice is served on the claimant.[9]

3.3 An increase to a Part 36 payment will be effective when notice of the increase is served on the claimant.[10]

(For service of the Part 36 payment notice see rule 36.6(3) and (4)).

3.4 A defendant who wishes to withdraw or reduce a Part 36 payment must obtain the court's permission to do so.

3.5 Permission may be obtained by making an application in accordance with Part 23 stating the reasons giving rise to the wish to withdraw or reduce the Part 36 payment.

Making a Part 36 payment

4.1 To make a Part 36 payment the defendant must file the following   **16.4** documents:

    (1) where that court is a county court or a district registry—

        (a) the Part 36 payment notice, and

        (b) the payment, usually a cheque made payable to Her Majesty's Paymaster General,

with the court, and

    (2) where that court is the Royal Courts of Justice—

        (a) the Part 36 payment notice with the court, and

        (b) the payment, usually a cheque made payable to the Accountant General of the Supreme Court, and

        (c) a sealed copy of the Claim Form,

        (d) the Court Funds Office form 100 with the Court Funds Office.

---

[5] See r.36.8(1).
[6] See r.36.8(3).
[7] Includes a respondent to a claim or issue.
[8] See r.36.3(1).
[9] See r.36.8(2).
[10] See r.36.8(4).

Part 36 offers and Part 36 payments — general provisions

16.5 5.1 A Part 36 offer or a Part 36 payment notice must:

(1) state that it is a Part 36 offer or that the payment into court is a Part 36 payment, and

(2) be signed by the offeror or his legal representative.[11]

5.2 The contents of a Part 36 offer must also comply with the requirements of rule 36.5(3), (5) and (6).

5.3 The contents of a Part 36 payment notice must comply with rule 36.6(2) and, if rule 36.23 applies, with rule 36.23(3).

5.4 A Part 36 offer or Part 36 payment will be taken to include interest unless it is expressly stated in the offer or the payment notice that interest is not included, in which case the details set out in rule 36.22(2) must be given.

5.5 Where a Part 36 offer is made by a company or other corporation, a person holding a senior position in the company or corporation may sign the offer on the offeror's behalf, but must state the position he holds.

5.6 Each of the following persons is a person holding a senior position:

(1) in respect of a registered company or corporation, a director, the treasurer, secretary, chief executive, manager or other officer of the company or corporation, and

(2) in respect of a corporation which is not a registered company, in addition to those persons set out in (1), the mayor, chairman, president, town clerk or similar officer of the corporation.

Clarification of Part 36 offer or payment

16.6 6.1 An offeree may apply to the court for an order requiring the offeror to clarify the terms of a Part 36 offer or Part 36 payment notice (a clarification order) where the offeror has failed to comply within 7 days with a request for clarification.[12]

6.2 An application for a clarification order should be made in accordance with Part 23.

6.3 The application notice should state the respects in which the terms of the Part 36 offer or Part 36 payment notice, as the case may be, are said to need clarification.

Acceptance of a Part 36 offer or payment

16.7 7.1 The times for accepting a Part 36 offer or a Part 36 payment are set out in rules 36.11 and 36.12.

7.2 The general rule is that a Part 36 offer or Part 36 payment made more than 21 days before the start of the trial may be accepted within 21 days after it was

---

[11] For the definition of legal representative see r.2.3.
[12] See r.36.9(1) and (2).

made without the permission of the court. The costs consequences set out in rules 36.13 and 36.14 will then come into effect.

7.3 A Part 36 offer or Part 36 payment made less than 21 days before the start of the trial cannot be accepted without the permission of the court unless the parties agree what the costs consequences of acceptance will be.

7.4 The permission of the court may be sought:

(1) before the start of the trial, by making an application in accordance with Part 23, and

(2) after the start of the trial, by making an application to the trial judge.

7.5 If the court gives permission it will make an order dealing with costs and may order that, in the circumstances, the costs consequences set out in rules 36.13 and 36.14 will apply.

7.6 Where a Part 36 offer or Part 36 payment is accepted in accordance with rule 36.11(1) or rule 36.12(1) the notice of acceptance must be sent to the offeror and filed with the court.

7.7 The notice of acceptance:

(1) must set out—
    (a) the claim number, and
    (b) the title of the proceedings,

(2) must identify the Part 36 offer or Part 36 payment notice to which it relates, and

(3) must be signed by the offeree or his legal representative (see paragraphs 6.5 and 6.6 above).

7.8 Where:

(1) the court's approval, or

(2) an order for payment of money out of court, or

(3) an order apportioning money in court—

    (a) between the Fatal Accidents Act 1976 and the Law Reform (Miscellaneous Provisions) Act 1934, or

    (b) between the persons entitled to it under the Fatal Accidents Act 1976,

is required for acceptance of a Part 36 offer or Part 36 payment, application for the approval or the order should be made in accordance with Part 23.

7.9 The court will include in any order made under paragraph 8.8 above a direction for;

(1) the payment out of the money in court, and

(2) the payment of interest.

7.10 Unless the parties have agreed otherwise:

(1) interest accruing up to the date of acceptance will be paid to the offeror, and

(2) interest accruing as from the date of acceptance until payment out will be paid to the offeree.

7.11 A claimant may not accept a Part 36 payment which is part of a defendant's offer to settle the whole of a claim consisting of both a money and a non-money claim unless at the same time he accepts the offer to settle the whole of the claim. Therefore:

(1) if a claimant accepts a Part 36 payment which is part of a defendant's offer to settle the whole of the claim, or

(2) if a claimant accepts a Part 36 offer which is part of a defendant's offer to settle the whole of the claim,

the claimant will be deemed to have accepted the offer to settle the whole of the claim.[13]

(See paragraph 9 below for the method of obtaining money out of court.)

Payment out of court

16.8　8.1 To obtain money out of court following acceptance of a Part 36 payment, the claimant should file a request for payment.[14]

8.2 The request for payment should contain the following details:

(1) where the party receiving the payment—

(a) is legally represented—
(i) the name, business address and reference of the legal representative, and
(ii) the name of the bank and the sort code number, the title of the account and the account number where the payment is to be transmitted, and

(2) where the party is acting in person—

(a) his name and address, and
(b) his bank account details as in (ii) above.

8.3 Where the request for payment is made to the Royal Courts of Justice, the claimant should also complete Court Funds Office form 201 and file it in the Court Funds Office.

8.4 Subject to paragraph 9.5(1) and (2), if a party does not wish the payment to be transmitted into his bank account or if he does not have a bank account, he may send a written request to the Accountant-General for the payment to be made to him by cheque.

8.5 Where a party seeking payment out of court has provided the necessary information, the payment:

(1) where a party is legally represented, must be made to the legal representative,

(2) if the party is not legally represented but is, or has been, in receipt of legal aid in respect of the proceedings and a notice to that effect has

---

[13] See r.36.4. This must be read in the light of the words introduced in r.36.4 by the Civil Procedure (Amendment) Rules 1999: see para. 15.4, above.

[14] In practice form N243.

been filed, should be made to the Legal Aid Board by direction of the court,

(3) where a person entitled to money in court dies without having made a will and the court is satisfied—

(a) that no grant of administration of his estate has been made, and
(b) that the assets of his estate, including the money in court, do not exceed in value the amount specified in any order in force under section 6 of the Administration of Estates (Small Payments) Act 1965,

may be ordered to be made to the person appearing to have the prior right to a grant of administration of the estate of the deceased, *e.g.* a widower, widow, child, father, mother, brother or sister of the deceased.

Foreign currency

9.1 Money may be paid into court in a foreign currency: **16.9**

(1) where it is a Part 36 payment and the claim is in a foreign currency, or
(2) under a court order.

9.2 The court may direct that the money be placed in an interest bearing account in the currency of the claim or any other currency.

9.3 Where a Part 36 payment is made in a foreign currency and has not been accepted within 21 days, the defendant may apply for an order that the money be placed in an interest bearing account.

9.4 The application should be made in accordance with Part 23 and should state:

(1) that the payment has not been accepted in accordance with rule 36.11, and
(2) the type of currency on which interest is to accrue.

Compensation recovery

10.1 Where a defendant makes a Part 36 payment in respect of a claim for a sum **16.10** or part of sum:

(1) which falls under the heads of damage set out in column 1 of Schedule 2 of the Social Security (Recovery of Benefits) Act 1997 in respect of recoverable benefits received by the claimant as set out in column 2 of that Schedule, and
(2) where the defendant is liable to pay recoverable benefits to the Secretary of State,

the defendant should obtain from the Secretary of State a certificate of recoverable benefits and file the certificate with the Part 36 payment notice.

10.2 If a defendant wishes to offer to settle a claim where he has applied for but not yet received a certificate of recoverable benefits, he may, provided that he makes a Part 36 payment not more than 7 days after he has received the certificate, make a Part 36 offer which will have the costs and other consequences set out in rules 36.13 and 36.20.

10.3 The Part 36 payment notice should state in addition to the requirements set out in rule 36.6(2):

(1) the total amount represented by the Part 36 payment (the gross compensation),

(2) that the defendant has reduced this sum by £   , in accordance with section 8 of and Schedule 2 to the Social Security (Recovery of Benefits) Act 1997, which was calculated as follows:

Name of benefit   Amount

and

(3) that the amount paid in, being the sum of £   is the net amount after the deduction of the amount of benefit.

10.4 On acceptance of a Part 36 payment to which this paragraph relates, a claimant will receive the sum in court which will be net of the recoverable benefits.

10.5 In establishing at trial whether a claimant has bettered or obtained a judgment more advantageous than a Part 36 payment to which this paragraph relates, the court will base its decision on the gross sum specified in the Part 36 payment notice.

General

16.11   11.1 Where a party on whom a Part 36 offer, a Part 36 payment notice or a notice of acceptance is to be served is legally represented, the Part 36 offer, Part 36 payment notice and notice of acceptance must be served on the legal representative.

11.2 In a claim arising out of an accident involving a motor vehicle on a road or in a public place:

(1) where the damages claimed include a sum for hospital expenses, and

(2) the defendant or his insurer pays that sum to the hospital under section 157 of the Road Traffic Act 1988,

the defendant must give notice of that payment to the court and all the other parties to the proceedings.

11.3 Money paid into court:

(1) as a Part 36 payment which is not accepted by the claimant, or

(2) under a court order,

will be placed in a basic account[15] (subject to paragraph 12.4 below) for interest to accrue.

11.4 Where money referred to in paragraph 12.3 above is paid in in respect of a child or patient it will be placed in a special investment account[16] for interest to accrue.

---

[15] See rule 26 of the Court Funds Rules 1987.
[16] See rule 26 as above.

(A practice direction supplementing Part 21 contains information about the investment of money in court in respect of a child or partient.)

(Practice directions supplementing Part 40 contain information about adjustment of the judgment sum in respect of recoverable benefits, and about structured settlements.)

(A practice direction supplementing Part 41 contains information about provisional damages awards.)

APPENDIX III

Part 36 Forms

**Notice of Payment into Court
(in settlement — Part 36)**

To the claimant ('s Solicitor)

In the	
Claim No	
Claimant incl. ref.	
Defendant incl. ref.	

Take notice the defendant   has paid £   (a further amount of £   )
into court in settlement of [the whole of] [part of] [a certain issue or issues in] your
claim *(give details below)*

The [part] [issue or issues] to which it relates is [are]: *(give details)*

[It is in addition to the amount of £   already paid into court on   ]

[It is not inclusive of interest].
[An additional amount of £   is offered for interest at the rate of £   per
from   to   ]

[It takes into account all [part] of the following counterclaim: *(give details of the
party and the part of the counterclaim to which the payment relates)*
                                                                                    ]

[It takes into account the interim payment(s) made in the following amount(s) on
the following date(s): *(give details)*
                                                                                    ]

For cases where the Social Security (Recovery of Benefits) Act 1997 applies
The gross amount of the compensation payment is £
The defendant has reduced this sum by £   in accordance with section 8 of
and Schedule 2 to the Social Security (Recovery of Benefits) Act 1997, which was
calculated as follows:

Type of benefit   Amount

Note: This notice will need to be modified where an offer of provisional
damages is made (CPR Part 36.7) and/or where it is made in relation to a mixed
(money and non-money) claim in settlement of the whole claim (CPR Part 36.4).

242A Notice of payment into court (in settlement) (4.99)

17.2 Notice of acceptance of payment into court (Part 36)

In the	
	Court
Claim No.	
Claimant's (including ref.)	
Defendant's (including ref.)	

Note:

If you wish to accept the payment made into court without needing the court's permission you should:
- send this completed notice to the defendant not more than 21 days after you received this notice
- and at the same time send a copy to the court

Delete as appropriate I accept the payment into court in settlement of (the whole of)(part of)*(certain issue(s) in)* my claim set out in the notice of payment into court received on *(insert date)*

I declare that it is:—

☐ not more than 21 days since I received the notice of payment into court

or

☐ more than 21 days since I received the notice and I have agreed the following costs with the other party(ies) *(give details)*

And I request payment of the money held in court to be made to

claimant's (solicitor's) full name and address (and ref)

name and address of bank	sort code

title of account	account number

Signed	Position held (If signing on behalf of a firm or company)

Date

N243   Notice of acceptance and request for payment (4.99)

APPENDIX IV

Extracts from Part 21 and Part 21 Practice Direction

PART 21

Compromise etc. by or on behalf of child or patient

21.10 — (1) Where a claim is made—   **18.1**

    (a) by or on behalf of a child or patient; or
    (b) against a child or patient,

no settlement, compromise or payment and no acceptance of money paid into court shall be valid, so far as it relates to the claim by, on behalf of or against the child or patient, without the approval of the court.

(2) Where—

    (a) before proceedings in which a claim is made by or on behalf of, or against a child or patient (whether alone or with any other person) are begun, an agreement is reached for the settlement of the claim; and
    (b) the sole purpose of proceedings on that claim is to obtain the approval of the court to a settlement or compromise of the claim,

the claim must—

    (i) be made using the procedure set out in Part 8 (alternative procedure for claims); and
    (ii) include a request to the court for approval of the settlement or compromise.

(Rule 48.5 contains provisions about costs where money is payable to a child or patient)

PART 21 PRACTICE DIRECTION

Settlement or compromise by or on behalf of a child or patient

18.2 6.1 Where a claim by or on behalf of a child or patient has been dealt with by agreement prior to the start of proceedings and only the approval of the court to the agreement is sought, the claim:

(1) must be made using the Part 8 procedure,
(2) must include a request for approval of the settlement or compromise, and
(3) in addition to the details of the claim, must set out the terms of the settlement or compromise or have attached to it a draft consent order in practice form N292.

6.2 In order to approve the settlement or compromise, the information concerning the claim that the court will require will include:

(1) whether and to what extent the defendant admits liability,
(2) the age and occupation (if any) of the child or patient,
(3) the litigation friend's approval of the proposed settlement or compromise, and
(4) in a personal injury case arising from an accident—

(a) the circumstances of the accident,
(b) any medical reports,
(c) where appropriate, a schedule of any past and future expenses and losses claimed and any other relevant information relating to personal injury as set out in the practice direction which supplements Part 16 (statements of case), and
(d) where considerations of liability are raised—
(i) any evidence or police reports in any criminal proceedings or in an inquest, and
(ii) details of any prosecution brought.

6.3 Applications for the approval of a settlement or compromise will normally be heard by a Master or district judge.

(For information about structured settlements see the practice direction on structured settlements supplementing Part 40 (judgments and orders))
(For information about provisional damages claims see Part 41 and the practice direction which supplements it)

Apportionment under the Fatal Accidents Act 1976

18.3 7.1 A judgment on or settlement in respect of a claim under the Fatal Accidents Act 1976 must be apportioned between the persons by or on whose behalf the claim has been brought.

7.2 Where a claim is brought on behalf of a dependent child or children, the money apportioned to any child must be invested on his behalf in accordance with rules 21.10 and 21.11 and paragraphs 8 and 9 below.

7.3 In order to approve an apportionment of money to a dependent child, the court will require the following information;

(1) the matters set out in paragraph 6.2(1), (2) above, and

(2) in respect of the deceased

    (a) where death was caused by an accident, the matters set out in paragraph 6.2(3)(a), (b) and (c) above, and

    (b) his future loss of earnings, and

(3) the extent and nature of the dependency.

APPENDIX V

Extracts from Part 26 and Part 26 Practice Direction

PART 26

Stay to allow for settlement of the case

19.1 26.4 — (1) A party may, when filing the completed allocation questionnaire, make a written request for the proceedings to be stayed(GL) while the parties try to settle the case by alternative dispute resolution(GL) or other means.
(2) Where—

> (a) all parties request a stay(GL) under paragraph (1); or
> (b) the court, of its own initiative, considers that such a stay would be appropriate,

the court will direct that the proceedings be stayed for one month.
(3) The court may extend the stay(GL) until such date or for such specified period as it considers appropriate.
(4) Where the court stays(GL) the proceedings under this rule, the claimant must tell the court if a settlement is reached.
(5) If the claimant does not tell the court by the end of the period of the stay(GL) that a settlement has been reached, the court will give such directions as to the management of the case as it considers appropriate.

PART 26 PRACTICE DIRECTION

Stay to allow for settlement of the case

19.2 3.1 Procedure for the parties to apply to extend the stay

(1) (a) The court will generally accept a letter from any party or from the solicitor for any party as an application to extend the stay under rule 26.4.

    (b) The letter should—
       (i) confirm that the application is made with the agreement of all parties, and
       (ii) explain the steps being taken and identify any mediator or expert assisting with the process.

(2) (a) An order extending the stay must be made by a judge.

    (b) The extension will generally be for no more than 4 weeks unless clear reasons are given to justify a longer time.

(3) More than one extension of the stay may be granted.

3.2 Position at the end of the stay if no settlement is reached.

(1) At the end of the stay the file will be referred to a judge for his directions.

(2) He will consider whether to allocate the claim to a track and what other directions to give, or may require any party to give further information or fix an allocation hearing.

3.3 Any party may apply for a stay to be lifted.

3.4 Position where settlement is reached during a stay.

Where the whole of the proceedings are settled during a stay, the taking of any of the following steps will be treated as an application for the stay to be lifted:

(1) an application for a consent order (in any form) to give effect to the settlement,

(2) an application for the approval of a settlement where a party is a person under a disability,

(3) giving notice of acceptance of money paid into court in satisfaction of the claim or applying for money in court to be paid out.

APPENDIX VI

Extract from Part 40 and Part 23 Practice Direction

PART 40

Consent judgments and orders

20.1   40.6 — (1) This rule applies where all the parties agree the terms in which a judgment should be given or an order should be made.

(2) A court officer may enter and seal^(GL) an agreed judgment or order if—

(a) the judgment or order is listed in paragraph (3);
(b) none of the parties is a litigant in person; and
(c) the approval of the court is not required by these Rules, a practice direction or any enactment before an agreed order can be made.

(3) The judgments and orders referred to in paragraph (2) are—

(a) a judgment or order for—
   (i) the payment of an amount of money (including a judgment or order for damages or the value of goods to be decided by the court); or
   (ii) the delivery up of goods with or without the option of paying the value of the goods or the agreed value.

(b) an order for—
   (i) the dismissal of any proceedings, wholly or in part;
   (ii) the stay^(GL) of proceedings on agreed terms, disposing of the proceedings, whether those terms are recorded in a schedule to the order or elsewhere;
   (iii) the stay^(GL) of enforcement of a judgment, either unconditionally or on condition that the money due under the judgment is paid by instalments specified in the order;
   (iv) the setting aside under Part 13 of a default judgment which has not been satisfied;
   (v) the payment out of money which has been paid into court;
   (vi) the discharge from liability of any party;
   (vii) the payment, assessment or waiver of costs, or such other provision for costs as may be agreed.

(4) Rule 40.3 (drawing up and filing of judgments and orders) applies to judgments and orders entered and sealed$^{(GL)}$ by a court officer under paragraph (2) as it applies to other judgments and orders.

(5) Where paragraph (2) does not apply, any party may apply for a judgment or order in the terms agreed.

(6) The court may deal with an application under paragraph (5) without a hearing.

(7) Where this rule applies—

    (a) the order which is agreed by the parties must be drawn up in the terms agreed;

    (b) it must be expressed as being 'By Consent';

    (c) it must be signed by the legal representative acting for each of the parties to whom the order relates or, where paragraph (5) applies, by the party if he is a litigant in person.

PART 23 PRACTICE DIRECTION

Consent orders

10.1 Rule 40.6 sets out the circumstances where an agreed judgment or order **20.2** may be entered and sealed.

10.2 Where all parties affected by an order have written to the court consenting to the making of the order a draft of which has been filed with the court, the court will treat the draft as having been signed in accordance with rule 40.6(7).

10.3 Where a consent order must be made by a judge (*i.e.* rule 40.6(2) does not apply) the order must be drawn so that the judge's name and judicial title can be inserted.

10.4 The parties to an application for a consent order must ensure that they provide the court with any material it needs to bve satisfied that it is appropriate to make the order. Subject to any rule or practice direction a letter will generally be acceptable for this purpose.

10.5 Where a judgment or order has been agreed in respect of an application or claim where a hearing date has been fixed, the parties must inform the court immediately. (Note that parties are reminded that under rules 28.4 and 29.5 the case management timetable cannot be varied by written agreement of the parties.)

APPENDIX VII

The New Millennium Tomlin Order

[TITLE OF CASE]

21.1 UPON [hearing Counsel for the parties] [hearing the solicitors for the parties] [reading the letter from the claimant's solicitor and the defendant's solicitor/ defendant in person]

AND UPON the parties having agreed terms of settlement

BY CONSENT

IT IS ORDERED that all further proceedings in this [matter/case] be stayed upon the terms set out in the [Schedule to this order] [document entitled "Settlement of Claim No. .... between [C] and [D]" dated .... and signed by (Counsel for each party) (the solicitors for each party) (the solicitor for C and the defendant in person), the original of which has been retained by (C's solicitors) and a copy of which has been retained by (D's solicitors) (D)][1] except for the purpose of enforcing those terms.

AND IT IS FURTHER ORDERED that either party may be permitted to apply to the court to enforce the terms upon which this [matter/case] has been stayed without the need to bring a new claim

AND IT IS RECORDED that the parties have agreed that any claim for breach of contract arising from an alleged breach of the terms set out in the [Schedule to this order] [the above-mentioned document] may, unless the Court orders otherwise, be dealt with by way of an application to the Court without the need to start a new claim[2]

AND IT IS FURTHER ORDERED [set out agreed order as to costs and include any Legal Aid taxation]

SCHEDULE

[set out terms of agreement here unless they are to be recorded on a separate document]

---

[1] If the parties wish to keep the terms of their agreement confidential by recording it elsewhere than in a Schedule to the order, which is part of a record that can be made public, then a formula such as that suggested will need to be adopted.

[2] This agreement is necessary if the parties wish to avoid the consequences of the case of *Hollingsworth v. Humphrey,* referred to in para. 9.16, above.

APPENDIX VIII

Precedents

A number of suggested Precedents follow. It is impossible to be exhaustive. **22.1**
Suitable modifications to those suggested will be required to accommodate different
offers.

1. General form of Part 36 offer relating to the whole claim made more than 21 **22.2**
days before the trial

2. General form of Part 36 offer relating to the whole claim made less than 21
days before the trial

3. General form of Part 36 offer relating to part of the claim made more than 21
days before the trial

4. General form of claimant's Part 36 offer relating to the whole of a money claim
made more than 21 days before the trial

5. General form of claimant's Part 36 offer relating to part of a money claim
made more than 21 days before the trial

6. General form of Part 36 offer as an open offer

7. General form of pre-action offer by a defendant in a money claim

8. General form of pre-action offer by a defendant in a non-money claim

9. Letter written by defendant in non-money claim who had made pre-action
offer to be sent to the claimant on the institution of proceedings

10. General form of claimant's pre-action offer in a money claim

11. General Form of Part 36 Payment Notice

12. Defendant's letter to claimant when making or increasing a Part 36 payment
during the trial

1. General form of Part 36 offer relating to the whole claim made more than 21 days before the trial[1]

22.3   Dear Sirs,   PART 36 OFFER

<u>C. v. D.</u>

We refer to the above matter in which we act for D.

Our client has instructed us to make the following offer to settle, the offer being made in accordance with Part 36, Civil Procedure Rules.

He offers to settle the whole claim on the terms that [set out precise terms offered]. [This offer takes into account/does not take into account his counterclaim for . . .]

This offer will remain open for acceptance for 21 days from the date you receive it. If your client gives notice of acceptance within that period, he will be entitled to his costs of the proceedings (assessed on the standard basis if not agreed) to the date of the service of that notice. If your client does not accept the offer within that period, then it can be accepted thereafter if we can agree the liability for the costs of the proceedings or the court gives permission.

[If our client's offer is accepted, or is permitted to be accepted by the court, we propose that it is embodied in a consent order/judgment in the terms set out in the enclosed draft or terms to like effect.][2]

Yours, etc.

---

[1] See Chap. 5.

[2] If an order beyond the rule-imposed Tomlin order is required, a paragraph to this effect would be sensible: para. 9.15, above.

2. General form of Part 36 offer relating to the whole claim made less than 21 days before the trial[1]

Dear Sirs,   PART 36 OFFER **22.4**

<u>C. v. D.</u>

We refer to the above matter in which we act for D.

Our client has instructed us to make the following offer to settle, the offer being made in accordance with Part 36, Civil Procedure Rules.

He offers to settle the whole claim on the terms that [set out precise terms offered]. [This offer takes into account/does not take into account his counterclaim for . . .]

Your client may accept it at any time before the trial begins if we can agree the liability for the costs of the proccedings or the court gives permission.

Our proposal in relation to the costs of the proceedings is [set out details]. If your client rejects that proposal, he can seek the permission of the court to accept the offer. Our client will contend that, if the court gives its permission, the order for costs should be [set out details]. However, our client makes it clear that he will abide by the decision of the court in this regard.

[If our client's offer is accepted, or is permitted to be accepted by the court, we propose that it is embodied in a consent order/judgment in the terms set out in the enclosed draft or terms to like effect.][2]

Yours, etc.

---

[1] See Chap. 5.
[2] If an order beyond the rule-imposed Tomlin order is required, a paragraph to this effect would be sensible: para. 9.15, above.

3. General form of Part 36 offer relating to part[1] of the claim made more than 21 days before the trial[2]

22.5   Dear Sirs,   PART 36 OFFER

C. v. D.

We refer to the above matter in which we act for D.

Our client has instructed us to make the following offer to settle, the offer being made in accordance with Part 36, Civil Procedure Rules.

Our client offers to settle [the part of the claim relating to . . .] on the following terms, namely, [set out details]. [The offer takes account/does not take account of our client's counterclaim.]

This offer will remain open for acceptance for 21 days from the date you receive it. If your client gives notice of acceptance within that period and at the time of serving it he abandons the balance of the claim, [our client accepts that your client will be entitled to his costs of the proceedings (assessed on the standard basis if not agreed) to the date of the service of that notice][3] [our client will apply to the court to seek a different order as to costs from that provided for in r.36.13(2). The order as to costs we propose is . . .][4]

If your client serves notice of acceptance within 21 days, but does not abandon the balance of his claim, we propose that the order for costs following the stay of the proceedings[5] is that [set out proposal]. If that proposal is not acceptable to your client, the court will have to decide the liability for costs.[6]

If your client does not accept the offer on either basis within that period, then it can be accepted thereafter if we can agree the liability for the costs of the proceedings or the court gives permission.

---

[1] This precedent could be adapted to make an offer to settle an "issue": paras 4.7-4.9.
[2] See Chap. 5.
[3] The usual order if C abandons the balance of his claim: r.36.13(2).
[4] This would be appropriate where, for example, the defendant considers that it would be unfair that C should have all the costs associated with the abandoned parts of his claim: see para. 9.5, above.
[5] r.36.15(3)(a).
[6] r.36.15(3)(b).

[If our client's offer is accepted, or is permitted to be accepted by the court, we propose that it is embodied in a consent order/judgment in the terms set out in the enclosed draft or terms to like effect.][7]

Yours, etc.

---

[7] If an order beyond the rule-imposed Tomlin order is required, a paragraph to this effect would be sensible: para. 9.15, above.

4. General form of claimant's Part 36 offer relating to the whole of a money claim made more than 21 days before the trial[1]

22.6   Dear Sirs,

PART 36 OFFER

C. v. D.

We refer to the above matter in which we act for C.

Our client has instructed us to make the following offer to settle, the offer being made in accordance with Part 36, Civil Procedure Rules.

As you know, our client's claim is for [damages arising from . . .] [the sum of £X arising from . . .] plus interest. He offers to settle the whole of his claim for the sum of £Y [which, for the avoidance of doubt, is inclusive of interest to 21 days from now.][2]

This offer will remain open for acceptance for 21 days from the date you receive it. If your client gives notice of acceptance within that period, our client will be entitled to his costs of the proceedings (assessed on the standard basis if not agreed) to the date of the service of that notice.[3]

If your client does not accept the offer within that period, then it can be accepted thereafter if we can agree the liability for the costs of the proceedings or the court gives permission.

[If your client does not accept this offer and is held liable at the trial for more, it would be our client's intention to rely on the provisions of r. 36.21.][4]

Yours, etc.

---

[1] See Chap. 5.

[2] These words are not strictly necessary since interest to the expiration of the 21-day period is deemed to be included: r.36.22(1). If interest is not included, but interest is demanded within the offer, details must be given: r.36.22(2). See para. 4.6, above.

[3] r.36.14.

[4] Again, these words are not strictly necessary because r.36.21 arises automatically once a claimant does better than his offer. However, there would be no harm in emphasising that reliance will be replaced upon it.

5.   General form of claimant's Part 36 offer relating to part[1] of a money claim made more than 21 days before the trial[2]

Dear Sirs,   PART 36 OFFER 22.7

C. v. D.

We refer to the above matter in which we act for C.

Our client has instructed us to make the following offer to settle, the offer being made in accordance with Part 36, Civil Procedure Rules.

As you know, our client's claim is for [damages arising from . . .] [the sum of £X arising from . . .] plus interest. One part of his overall claim relates to [give details]. He offers to settle that part of his claim for the sum of £Z [which, for the avoidance of doubt, is inclusive of interest to 21 days from now.][3]

This offer will remain open for acceptance for 21 days from the date you receive it. If your client gives notice of acceptance within that period, we propose that the order for costs following the stay of the proceedings[4] is that [set out proposal]. If that proposal is not acceptable to your client, the court will have to decide the liability for costs.[5]

If your client does not accept the offer within that period, then it can be accepted thereafter if we can agree the liability for the costs of the proceedings or the court gives permission.

[If your client does not accept this offer and is held liable at the trial for more, it would be our client's intention to rely on the provisions of r. 36.21.][6]

Yours, etc.

---

[1] paras 4.7–4.9.
[2] See Chap. 5.
[3] These words are not strictly necessary since interest to the expiration of the 21-day period is deemed to be included: r.36.22(1). If interest is not included, but interst is demanded within the offer, details must be given: r.36.22(2). See para. 4.6, above.
[4] r.36.15(3)(a).
[5] r.36.15(3)(b).
[6] Again, these words are not strictly necessary because r.36.21 arises automatically once a claimant does better than his offer. However, there would be no harm in emphasising that reliance will be placed upon it. It should, however, be noted that, whilst r.36.21 is not precluded from operation when *part only* of a claim forms the subject of the claimant's offer, its practical implementation may generally be difficult in cases other than where the offer is for settlement of the *whole* claim.

6. General form of Part 36 offer as an open offer

22.8   Dear Sirs,   PART 36 OFFER

<u>C. v. D.</u>

We refer to the above matter in which we act for D.

Our client has instructed us to make the following offer to settle, the offer being made in accordance with Part 36, Civil Procedure Rules. We would draw attention to the fact that it is our client's wish that this offer should be treated as an open offer. For the avoidance of doubt, therefore, we make it plain that our client waives any privilege attaching to the offer by reason of r.36.19(1).[1]

[continue with substance of offer]

Yours, etc.

---

[1] See para. 2.3 and para. 2.6 *et seq.*

7. General form of pre-action offer by a defendant in a money claim[1]

Dear Sirs,

C. v. D.

We refer to the above matter in which we act for D.

Your client has intimated a claim for [damages arising from . . .] [£X arising from . . .].

Our client offers to settle the whole claim in the sum of £Y [inclusive of interest until 21 days hence] [exclusive of interest which is offered at the rate of . . .% p.a. from . . . to . . .].[2] He also offers to pay your client's reasonable costs up to 21 days from the date you receive this offer.

This offer remains open for 21 days after you receive it. [It takes account/does not take account of the counterclaim our client has intimated.]

If your client does not accept the offer, but in due course begins proceedings in relation to this matter, it will be our client's intention to pay the above-mentioned sum into court within 14 days of the service of the claim form so that the provisions of r.36.10 will apply.

Yours, etc.

---

[1] Chap. 3.
[2] These details are required to ensure that the offer complies with Part 36 (see para. 3.3 above): r.36.5(3)(c).

8. General form of pre-action offer by a defendant in a non-money claim[1]

22.10   Dear Sirs,   PRE-ACTION OFFER

<u>C. v. D.</u>

We refer to the above matter in which we act for D.

Your client has intimated a claim for [set out details].

Our client offers to settle the whole claim on the terms/basis that [set out details of offer]. [If this offer is accepted, we would suggest that a formal deed is executed so that the boundary is henceforth clearly defined.][2]

He also offers to pay your client's reasonable costs up to 21 days from the date you receive this offer [together with the reasonable costs of preparing and executing the above-mentioned deed].

This offer remains open for 21 days after you receive it. [It takes account/does not take account of the counterclaim our client has intimated.]

[OR - This offer remains open on the terms we have mentioned for 21 days from the date you receive it. Should your client elect not to accept it within that period, it will remain open until proceedings are begun except that our client would require payment of his reasonable costs incurred after 21 days have elapsed from the date you receive it.] [If the offer is not accepted before proceedings are begun, it will remain open for acceptance thereafter, but only with the permission of the court. We would invite the court to give permission only on the basis that our client's costs from 21 days after you receive this offer should be met by your client on an indemnity basis.][3]

Yours, etc.

---

[1] Chap. 3. There will not be many claims which are purely "non-money". However, a claim for a declaration about a disputed boundary where there is no additional claim for damages is one example.

[2] This would probably be sensible in a boundary dispute.

[3] If the offeror wants to put his pre-action offer on virtually the same footing as a pre-action offer in a money claim, a paragraph along these lines would be sensible: see para. 3.15 above. Another alternative is to make a pre-action offer as shown in the above Precedent down to the part in square brackets starting OR and then to write a letter as shown in Precedent 9, below.

9. Letter written by defendant in non-money claim who had made pre-action offer to be sent to the claimant on the institution of proceedings[1]

Dear Sirs, 22.11

C. v. D.

We refer to our pre-action offer dated . . . which your client did not accept within the time given for acceptance.

Now that he has instituted proceedings, may we state that the offer can be treated as open for acceptance with the permission of the court within r. 36.10(4)(a). We would invite the court to give permission only on the basis that our client's costs from 21 days after you received the pre-action offer should be met by your client on an indemnity basis.[2]

Yours, etc.

---

[1] See Precedent 8 above and para. 3.15 of the text.
[2] Any other suggestion as to costs could, of course, be made, but this is thought to be the most likely suggestion in the situation. At the end of the day, it will be for the court to decide.

10. General form of claimant's pre-action offer in a money claim

22.12   Dear Sirs,   PRE-ACTION OFFER

C. v. D.

We refer to the above matter in which we act for C.

Our client has intimated a claim for [damages arising from . . .] [£X arising from . . .].

Our client is prepared to, and offers to, settle the whole claim in the sum of £Y [inclusive of interest until 21 days hence] [exclusive of interest which he offers to accept at the rate of . . .% p.a. from . . . to . . .].[1]

He would, of course, expect that his reasonable costs up to 21 days from the date you receive this offer would be met.

This offer remains open for 21 days after you receive it. [It takes account/does not take account of the counterclaim your client has intimated.]

Should our client's offer not be accepted and it becomes necessary for him to commence proceedings, it will be his intention to rely on r.36.21 if the award of the court exceeds his present offer.

Yours, etc.

---

[1] These details are required to ensure that the offer complies with Part 36 (see para. 3.3 above): r.36.5(3)(c).

11. General Form of Part 36 Payment Notice[1]

[standard parts]

Take notice that the defendant [has paid £ .... into court] [has paid a **22.13** further amount of £........ into court]

This payment is in settlement of [the whole of]* *or* [part of]* *or* [a certain issue *or* certain issues in]* your claim.

[The [part] [issue *or* issues]* to which it relates is/are: (*give details*)

]

[It is in addition to the sum of £................ paid into court on.....................]

[It is not inclusive of interest. An additional amount of £.......... is offered in respect of interest and has been paid into court.[2] This has been calculated at the rate of .... for the period from .... to .... on the sum of £ .... (*or such other details as may be appropriate*)]

[It takes into account all/part of the following counterclaim: *details to be given*]

[It takes into account the interim payment(s) made in the following sum(s) on the following date(s) — (*give details*)

]

For cases where the Social Security (Recovery of Benefits) Act 1997 applies:

The gross amount of the compensation payment is £ ....

---

[1] This notice will require modification where an offer of provisional damages is made (r.36.7) and/or where it is made in relation to a mixed (money and non-money) claim and r.36.4 relied on. It will also require modification when the sum paid into court is the same as, and relates to, a pre-action offer: para. 3.9, above. Words to the effect that the sum is paid into court to comply with r.36.10(3) should appear prominently on the Part 36 payment notice.

[2] r.36.22(2) requires the notice to specify if interest is *offered* and "the amount offered, the rate or rates offered and the period or periods for which it is offered." Since the offer represents an offer in respect of a money claim (*i.e.* the claim for interest), the sum must be paid into court. It will, of course, be open to the claimant to accept the principal sum, but not the sum in respect of interest which could then be the subject of an adjudication by the court.

The defendant has reduced this sum by £ .... in accordance with section 8 of and Schedule 2 to the Social Security (Recovery of Benefits) Act 1997, which was calculated as follows:

Type of benefit	Amount

DATED, etc.

*To be chosen as applicable.

12. Defendant's letter to claimant when making or increasing a Part 36 payment during the trial[1]

Dear Sirs,   22.14

C. v. D.

We refer to the trial taking place between the above parties.

We enclose with this letter a Part 36 payment notice in which we give notice that our client has paid a further £............. into court.

Our client's appraisal of this case has changed with the recent disclosure of the documents relating to .... Had he seen those documents earlier he would have taken a different view on the merits of your client's claim.

Because it is this late disclosure that has prompted the further payment into court, we do not consider it right for your client to have his full costs to date. Our offer is, therefore, that your client should have his costs to .... and that there should be no order as to costs thereafter. If your client agrees to this, the full Part 36 payment can be accepted without seeking the court's permission. [We would propose an order in accordance with the enclosed draft.]

If your client does not agree that order as to costs, he can, of course, still seek the court's permission to accept the sum offered. If he does this, we will be contending that the permission should only be granted on the basis of the order for costs proposed above.

Since the trial is in progress and your client has access to his legal advisers, our proposal in relation to costs will be available until the conclusion of tomorrow's proceedings. If the payment is not accepted on the above basis by then, we will be seeking an order for our client's costs thereafter on the indemnity basis.

Yours, etc.

---

[1] See para. 10.12.

INDEX